DEREK GARDE

Y0-DDO-224

experiencing

MO

the principles of Jesus

MEN

in a life-changing manner

TUM

Momentum
Copyright 2016 by Derek Garde

Thank you for buying an authorized edition of this book and for complying with copyright laws by not reproducing, scanning, or distributing any part of Momentum in any form without permission.

Scripture quotations are taken from The Holy Bible, New International Version®, NIV® Copyright © 1973, 1978, 1984, 2011 by Biblica, Inc.® Used by permission. All rights reserved worldwide.

Cover Design by Jared Younger
Interior Design by Renee Evans

Funded and produced by BookRally:
www.bookrally.com

BR
BOOK**RALLY**
ISBN: 978-1-942306-77-1

Printed in the United States

DEDICATION

Dedicated to my parents, who poured their lives and souls into bringing out the best in us boys. Thanks for your endless love, teaching, wisdom, and encouragement. You taught us what life looks like chasing after Jesus and holding nothing back. This book is for you.

CONTENTS

INTRODUCTION   1

AUTHOR'S NOTE   3

1.   Made for More   9

2.   God Doesn't Need   17

3.   Identity Crisis   29

4.   Proving Grounds   49

5.   The Heart of God   63

6.   Brave the Unknown   73

7.   People Are People   89

8.   Authentic Community   105

9.   288 Square Inches   117

10. Discipline Breeds Freedom   127

11. There Should Be a Difference   139

12. Stories Worth Telling   151

INTRODUCTION

Twenty-four years old and I feel like I've lived 2 to 3 times the amount of life that most people experience in a lifetime. From selling shoes at Converse to working as a registered nurse at one of the nation's top pediatric institutes in the cardiac intensive care unit, life has been a wild ride. Traveling on the backs of elephants, to scooter rides in Florence, to motorbike rides on the dirt roads of Tanzania, and bicycle taxis in Nicaragua, life has been constant movement. Throughout it all I've never stopped searching for meaning and a higher purpose to this life. Along the way I found a deeper side of God, of life, and of love. These principles have guided my thinking and continue to propel me forward, gaining momentum with each passing day.

I'm a kid with a heart, a willingness to learn, and the ability to see beyond what is and to envision what could be. I would sacrifice anything to make a difference; this book is just the beginning.

This is my heart on paper.

This is my story.

AUTHOR'S NOTE

"I have come that they may have life and life to the full."[1]

Life to the full, life as it was intended to be lived, an abundance of adventures and daring escapes along with heart wrenching stories of sacrifice and love. This book is somewhat of a memoir, a collection of stories and experiences that have shaped my view of God, Christianity, life and, ultimately, love. It stems from the basic premise of taking Jesus at his word and asking, What would happen if we, who are God's children, his nation, his kingdom, his hands and feet, the representatives of Jesus, physically and mentally took hold of the principles that Jesus laid bare by manifesting those principles into our everyday lives? What would happen if we truly lived out what we confessed to believe in? I cannot but help to imagine how radical a place that would be where people developed into who they were designed to become: people made fully alive by following after their heart's desires and passions as God intended. This book is about the transformation of a mediocre, mundane life into a daring adventure, a life fully worth living.

---

[1] John 10:10

It's easy to write a book about how to be successful in seven steps by starting new habits or abstaining from certain activities, but I don't think Jesus had that in mind. Out of all the recorded conversations we have of Jesus, he never gave us overbearing rules to live by; he gave us stories. We connect deeply with story. Story is one of the greatest teaching tools we know of. Jesus gave us principles as a guidebook, instead of a set standard of rules and strict daily disciplines. He taught principles, not rules, to govern our thoughts and actions since he made each one of us unique in his image and each of us has a different story to live.

It's been thousands of years and yet human nature is essentially the same. Now we just have fancy gadgets to distract us, and things are more convenient than ever, yet we still long for a deeper meaning. Everyone is desperately looking for meaning. Our culture is more lost than we have ever been before. We long for wholeness and meaning, usually only finding temporary satisfaction and fleeting pleasure. I pray God can use this book to open your eyes to discover Jesus breaking through the silence in the everyday situations, demonstrating how to experience him more wholly during the common pursuits of daily life.

God didn't call us to live a boring, average or dull life—he called us to a life as he intended it to be before the fall of mankind: a life full of thrilling escapades and intricate meaning. He destined us for life as we've never imagined it before—life with no shame, no pain, no humiliation, no fear—a life of pure satisfaction in God alone, experiencing all he created for us to enjoy. It's such a powerful picture that cannot be put into words or experienced on this side of eternity. Out of the overflowing goodness of God's nature, he occasionally gives us glimpses into what could be by letting us experience a deeper part of who he is. God paints this picture of eternity in various adventures, such as traveling the world, starting a family, the joy in creating, the ability to learn, when we cross an experience off our bucket list, every sunset and sunrise, and so much more.

A daring adventure is out there, calling us to more than a mundane life, and that's exactly what Jesus has called us toward also. God didn't just give us salvation and desert us to figure out the rest. He desires every part of us and will take our brokenness and fill in the pieces to craft our life stories into an outstanding work of art. With Jesus, this life can be complete and meaningful once again. He is the master of redemption, the Creator who never makes mistakes, the Lover who does no wrong, the true King who is worthy, and the Author of life.

Life is something that we try our best to control. We plan, we grasp with all our strength and do everything in our power to maintain this equilibrium of balance. When we feel like we control life, we are under the false assumption that we are safe and free from harm. It's only when we break that mindset of false security that we can open ourselves to the freedom that Jesus calls us toward. It's through the dark nights and hard times and the many uncertainties in life that I have matured the most in my faith. Often in those moments of doubt is where I find God working the most—when I come to the end of myself. Where my strength ends and my weakness and brokenness are surrounding me, sitting on the edge with nothing left to give, God makes purpose out of the emptiness of my life. My weaknesses show the power of God in my life. I pray this book has a divine impact and marks the beginnings of change in your life's story.

In this pursuit of something bigger, we're going to ask the difficult questions. These questions dig beneath the surface and uncover who we are and what Jesus had to say about life, and why the life we've been given is worth living with excellence. It's a call to the action-minded—to grow and develop into more than we currently are. This book isn't intended to be an easy read; it isn't afraid of the reality of life, painting the good along with the bad. Momentum is about finding the truth—no matter the cost. Not only discovering the truth, but about taking the truth and applying what we discover to our daily lives. It's not enough to simply say we believe something; there's no power in that. Power comes through action, action comes through belief, and belief comes through a questioning attitude, life experiences, and constant learning.

I don't claim to have all the answers or an incredible sense of life or even have everything together, because honestly I don't. I strive my best to keep my eyes open and focused on Jesus while learning from the experiences I've had the opportunity to be a part of. I'm broken and I've been to dark and lost places; I've seen things and done things I can't rid my mind of, but I know that Jesus restores and actively redeems. His grace is sufficient to all who turn to him. He makes beautiful things out of shattered lives and actively resuscitates dying hearts. Out of the darkness the light of Jesus shines through.

I've observed the reality of simplistic thoughts put into practice, which produce sustainable change over time. For people who want to do big things, accomplish something more than the American dream, and influence culture—keep on reading. Together, we can discover a life that has significant meaning while impacting the world around us. God works in us and through us to produce the change around us. Radically simplistic, but a lot of things Jesus has revealed to me are just that—simple commands and instructions on how to live a better story. It's about love in action, not just in thought. It's a lifestyle of sacrifice and love, leaving us vulnerable and therefore valuable, while writing an incredible story along the way.

When we start to make these small fundamental changes in our thinking, it is incredible how rapidly our lives are amped up. It sends a jolt to the system. That charge sets other changes off down the conduction system in other aspects of our lives, and before we know it, things are radically different. We cannot help but see life differently. Tiny shifts in our thinking will open up opportunities that will exponentially change more thinking patterns until we have neurons firing off in every direction.

This book is about growing in step with God and achieving a higher performance in all aspects of life based on what Jesus says and who Jesus is. The goal of this book is for us to realize and understand what a person's potential in life can ultimately look like when we pursue Jesus wholeheartedly. What Jesus said and the actions he performed and the underlying reasons are critical components of the vital principles we aim to chase. This isn't a Sunday school lesson; this is life. I don't want this to be an easy book and when you put it down say, "That was nice," and keep living the exact same way. I desire for this book to challenge you to grow more intimate in your relationship with God. If it doesn't accomplish that, I hope this never finds its way into your hands.

Welcome to the momentum.

1 MADE FOR MORE

Deep within us we all have this unquenchable thirst for more. It seems like we're born with this desire, a striving to know there is more to our lives than what is seen or explained by science. It stems from the basic premise of taking Jesus at his word and asking, what would happen if we, who are God's children, his nation, his kingdom, his hands and feet, the representatives of Jesus, physically and mentally took hold of the principles that Jesus laid bare by manifesting those principles into our everyday lives?

I don't think I'm stretching to state that we've all felt this way before. I would go as far as to say that we're missing out on what God created us for. We've been selling ourselves short on what God has promised, what God has designed for life, and now we're paying the price. Our families are paying the price, society is paying the price, and our churches are paying the price for taking the easy way out and not challenging ourselves to become more than we currently are.

When you experience God moving, you realize that life doesn't have to be lived this way. We can be more. We were created for more—more than we've dreamed of or imagined, and that's where God's heart is. He desires to take us deeper, to show us more, and to give us life.

I've always said I don't want to watch TV when I can live a life worthy of television itself. Once you've experienced the real thing, anything that isn't authentic doesn't make the cut. It takes intentionality to live a life that is different from the mob of society. God desires more for our lives than we can even imagine for our own. God didn't design us with the mentality to survive, but the ability to flourish and make a difference with the resources he has given to us. You have a unique role in this life, and you are the only one who can play your part. We are collectively part of a bigger story.

I'm not sure where you are on your own walk with God, but I do know our view of God is said to be the most important aspect of our lives. Whether you are a believer in Jesus or not, you have a view of God in one aspect or another. You believe he exists or he doesn't, or you're stuck somewhere in between. We all hold a worldview, our way of seeing the world, our framework for the surroundings we find ourselves in. One of my favorite quotes is by A.W. Tozer, who said, "What comes into our minds when we think about God is the most important thing about us."

We shape the world we live in, not by how it is, but by how we perceive it to be. Our perception creates our reality. That doesn't mean that is how reality actually is, but the way we believe it is. It all stems from our thoughts and beliefs. Our thinking patterns are critical to living a story that matters. Our thoughts about God are the most significant aspects of who we are. These thoughts will dictate the unfolding of every event in our story. Our beliefs provide the context for where we belong and how we relate to the bigger story of life.

How we view God is the most vital part of our lives. Everything in our life, conscious and subconscious, is related to the way we choose to view God. If we see God as an angry authority figure in our lives, we begin to live that out by trying to please "The Man," continually striving not to do anything wrong or cross boundaries that would upset him and bring the hammer down on us. If we view God as the grandfather figure swinging his life away on the porch, weak and humble, I suppose we would view him as rather boring. As if perhaps at one point in time God did something, but is now incapable of doing anything relevant in our modern day and age. However, when we view God as he actually is life transforms instantaneously. The right view of God will dramatically change our everyday lives.

Personally, most days I view God as another number on my to-do list. If I'm lucky he makes the top three. Unfortunately, some days he doesn't even make the cut. My life shouldn't be lived that way. God shouldn't even be on a to-do list; he deserves more than that. If my view of God changes, my life will also change in a drastic manner. My actions reflect my beliefs. If you want to see where my beliefs are, then just watch my actions. We live what we believe. When my thoughts and actions are negative in nature, I can tell you almost 100 percent of the time it's because I haven't been spending quality time with God. What we believe in life is made evident by our actions.

The difference between people who say they are Christians and those who are striving after Jesus is that one knows the heart of God and the other doesn't. Knowing someone's heart makes all the difference. When we know the heart of God, life isn't about doing more; rather it's about becoming more. Our lives are shaped differently.

When we have a proper vision of God, our lives will never be the same. We physically, mentally, and spiritually cannot remain the same. Our lives will be shaped and moved into more dangerous territory because we have seen who God is and what his heart is about. He's tested my faith and I've seen him come through time after time, slowly advancing me deeper into his presence where I can let go of fear, fully relying on God to deliver and redeem my situation. It's only because I know the heart of God that I can place all of my life into his hands.

A life that is marked by God is a life where God is the exact middle of the circle, the bullseye of life. All of who we are should flow from his presence and through his divine perspective. God is more than another number on the list. We as a society have boxed God up and given him a few minutes throughout the day and maybe a Sunday morning here and there. God isn't just another priority or obligation to fulfill; he should be the middle of it all. God plays a part in every single aspect of our lives. Everything should flow from our identity that God has distinctly given to each one of us. And if you think God is boring, you haven't met him yet.

There is no distinction between the sacred and the secular to God. We are the ones who make that distinction and draw that line. We, as people, like boxes. A box for this and a box for that, simplifying and breaking down the hours of the day to schedule more things in order to increase efficiency. I get that. I do that for everything. I tend to put God in his own little box and maybe, maybe, on a good day give him an hour here or an hour there.

But there is no compartmentalizing with God. Take God out of the box, because the box will always be too small. The box can't handle who God is. All of life should overflow from our relationship with God and the abundance of love pouring out of that divine relationship. Our lives will radically change when we understand the nature of who God is and who we were created to be. We will continue to limit the energy in our lives if we continue to limit the abilities of God.

Remember back in grade school biology learning about symbiosis, the long-term interaction between two different species? The term symbiosis just means living together. The three types of relationships of symbiosis are parasitism, commensalism, and mutualism. Parasitism is an association between the two different species where the symbiont benefits and the host is harmed from the relationship. Commensalism is an association between the two where one species enjoys the benefits, and the other is not significantly affected either way. The third type of symbiosis where both species benefit from the relationship is called mutualism.

Often, I think we view our relationship with God as parasitism or at best commensalism. Of course, we don't use those terms to think of our relationship with God, but if we think of it like this I think that's exactly what we'll find. We either think that we have to sacrifice and God benefits out of our misery or service, or God sacrifices and we benefit out of his sacrifice for us.

Commonly, we feel like we have to sacrifice to please God, and yet he sacrificed to give us what we needed and desperately desired: himself. It's rare to think that our relationship with

God is mutualistic because we get what we desire, which is love and a deeper meaning in life, and God also benefits because he gets what he desires, which is us. It didn't just happen, God intentionally planned the redemption of his people and made the sacrifices necessary to reconcile us back to himself.

Don't make the mistake of thinking our relationship to God is parasitic—because it's not. It's far from that.

We were made for more than boxes and a limited perspective on God. I know that Jesus is the answer for those missing links in our thinking. Everything in life is rooted in the truth that Jesus is the answer. I know we go through difficult circumstances, heartbreaks, mountain-top experiences, and a full range of emotions and trials—and Jesus is the answer to it all. All of life stems from this, even when we can't see it—especially when we can't see it. I wrote this out of my own struggles, my own search for meaning. I knew there was more to life than the broken emptiness I found all around me. I could feel there was more to what I was living. This is a small glimpse of what I've found along my journey to writing a better story.

And I realize it sounds simplistic and naive to say that Jesus is the answer to everything. I haven't found a situation where he isn't. After I dug deep enough, thought long enough, all I uncovered was that at the root of every issue is the lack of Jesus, his love, and an eternal perspective on the issue.

I've always asked the questions "How does this make a difference? Why does this matter?" The following is a small glimpse of the answers I've learned so far. I'll be the first to tell you I still have a lot to learn, a lot of experiences to live through, and more things to feel. I've always searched for the deeper meaning in life. I think God gave me a few of the answers I was looking for.

There is more to life than we can imagine. There is something eternal on the line. There is so much at stake. Our story matters. We matter. Life itself matters. Life was intended for more than survival. It was meant to be lived full-heartedly. Everything in life has climaxed to this point. The good, the bad, the light, and the darkness all serve a deeper purpose.

Numerous times we are told that we are mistakes, random happenings of science, an accident, just a collection of cells, tissues, and organs, but that's not the whole story. Life is full of intricate meaning. Life is full of vitality. This world needs you. We need each other.

When we intentionally look into our lives, we can find and cut out what isn't necessary, giving us more resources for what is vital. The life God called you to will look vastly different than anyone else's. You don't have to start a non-profit, sell all you own and move to South America, or even do more things. Living a life with purpose and adventure is a mindset of following after God no matter the cost. If you're called to those things, that's great, and you should do that. Many people aren't called to those things, but that doesn't mean you're not chasing after God; he just has different plans for you. Adventure is a mindset, and God has so much more for your life than what is visible at this moment in time. You were made for more.

2 *GOD DOESN'T NEED*

God doesn't need. God doesn't need you. God doesn't need me. This is one of the most critical concepts to grasp in our deeper search for meaning and fulfillment in life. One of the most devastating perceptions of our generation is the lack of knowledge and belief that God is all he claims to be. We can sing Sunday after Sunday about how great our God is, but if we don't actually believe the words coming out of our own mouths or the lyrics on the screen—we are just wasting our breath and missing a prime opportunity to sleep in.

One of the reasons I've always been attracted to the action sports scene is the rebellious nature and attitude within that culture. They constantly ask the question "Why?" and if they don't see a valid reason behind the question, they don't conform. They don't do it just to do it, and they don't seem to care what you think either way. They shrug it off, keep skating and roll away from the dogma and drama.

Society may see it as radical or unable to cope with authority, and that could partially be it, but another reason is that they pursue freedom and something more than the mundane. The level of evolution sweeping through the action sports scene is unmatched. Surfing has completely evolved from just a few short years ago with the incorporation of airs, including 540s and double-grab backflips. At my local snowboarding hill, kids are pulling off triple corks, which is essentially a triple backflip with a 540 thrown in. These are tricks that pros, a few years back, wouldn't even have been doing in the X-Games. Now it's an everyday trick. Progression is happening because people, who aren't afraid of making mistakes and failing, continue to push forward.

It's because they're not afraid of boundaries; they're not afraid to push until they break, and then continue pushing. Sure, they didn't land the trick, and ended up in the hospital for a few weeks doing physical therapy, but to them, every second is worth it to push past what's previously been done. It's a challenge. The progression of the action sport world is astounding. They thrive on pushing past the impossible, and the crazy thing is—it shows.

Contrast that to my life. Many days I pray the same prayers and sing the same songs—yet without power or force behind the words because I've lost the true focus of who God is, what he's previously done, and what he is capable of doing. I've lost God in the small, ordinary happenings of daily life. Sure, we hear and read about how powerful God is and how great God can be, but it's hard to realize that the same God we read about in the Bible is the same God who is still at work today and is weaving our very beings together. It's hard to keep that perspective. Maybe we go on a mission trip or make it to Passion Conference or whatever else gets your spiritual engine revving, but eventually we lose that fire. We lose that intensity because we lose perspective of who God is.

It's hard to keep the view that the Jesus who conquered death is the same Jesus who is pursuing me day in and day out. The same God who created the universe with only his words is the same God who cares about the daily happenings of my life. Maybe we lose it because we have parking tickets to pay, dishes to do, places to go, homework to finish before the midnight deadline, or exams coming up. It's easy to lose divine perspective because we lose sight of the fact that we are spiritual beings and that we are made for more than a comfortable life.

One of the most profound perspectives that we've lost completely is the aspect of God's needlessness. I'm not sure if it's because we desire to feel good and we desire to contribute to what God is doing and therefore we are needed in our own finite sense. We have this idea that we are absolutely crucial to God's plan and purpose in the world. We're not. God doesn't need. God doesn't need you. God doesn't need me.

If God needed, then he would cease to be God. You see, God was perfectly complete in and of himself. The Trinity was one and three at the same time. The most perfect community and the most self-sustaining being ever. He didn't need to create earth or create animals and humans to roam about in order to feel powerful and in charge of something, to be the mastermind, to be the head general, to be "The Man." God knew exactly who he was; he didn't have to prove that to anyone, anything, or even himself. He was absolutely content in and of himself—100 percent complete, not lacking anything from eternity past to the present and forever more, God will never need, will never be found wanting, and will never be lacking.

After attempting to realize that we actually aren't needed by God to accomplish his goal or purpose, we might ask, "Why in the world did he create us then if he didn't need us or have an inherent use for us?" The simple answer is, God created us as an expression of his love. He did this whole planet Earth thing just to reveal who he is and what he is about. God created us to experience the abundant, perfect love of the Trinity. God is love; it is in the core of who God is that he was more than willing to create fallible human beings to enjoy and cherish his love. It's God's very nature to be the giver and the sustainer of life.

God didn't need us then and he doesn't need us now. He was so generous that even though he knew we would eventually turn our backs on him, God already had a plan in place to redeem us from our wrongdoings and bring us back into perfect harmony, through the atoning sacrifice of Jesus Christ. Jesus was willing from the beginning of time to sacrifice himself in order to bring the very human beings God created, who scarred God's heart by turning our backs on the giver of life who only had the best intentions for us, back into right standing with God. That's who God is. He's not some chump on the side of the road begging for our time and money. He's more than we could ever fathom. Anything good you've found in this life is simply a reflection of his qualities and character. The most vivid everyday reminder I've experienced is setting aside time to gaze at the sunrise and the sunset blasting radiant colors that make everything they touch come alive, which in turn reflect and boast of the artistic hand of God.

This all stems back to the fact that God doesn't need us. God simply desires to be with us, fully engaged and active in the deepest love affair known to man—that's why he created us. He had the purest motive possible—our own happiness and perfect fulfillment, which is to his own glory. When we view God in that light, it will constantly produce the most impactful changes in our lives. We cannot remain the same because through this realization we are given a deeper sense of understanding, purpose, life and love. Everything changes when we develop the proper perspective. We don't need to produce in order for God to tell us we're enough; we've always been enough for him.

This concept plays out in my life in a past relationship I was heavily involved in at the time. This relationship displayed this concept with precision; I was "needed" by my girlfriend. I had something that she needed, and I was wanted because of it. I had this constant pressure to perform for the sake of the relationship. I had to compensate for her insecurities and her shortcomings and try to validate her identity. That's a lot of weight to carry. I knew there would be major consequences if I failed to produce that. So I provided all those things, and it was exhausting and overwhelming. And it was far from healthy.

Honestly, it feels good to be needed. Doesn't it? It brings us a sense of meaning of what we thought we were longing for. If we are able to fulfill someone's needs, that's always a good thing, right? Some days it was a hassle, but other days it brought an astounding sense of accomplishment to be able to provide for someone else and fulfill the longing to be needed.

We settle for finding pleasure from being needed because we do not have the experience of being desired by someone to compare it with. There is a difference between being needed for what you can contribute and being desired for who you are. When we only feel the sense of being needed, we sell out and we take that instead of holding out for something better.

The difference between being needed and desired is life giving.

When we are needed, that means we have to continually produce. We have to give the other person in the relationship what they desire or else it will fall apart. How many times do we see this in what our society calls love? Being needed isn't a solid foundation for a relationship. Over time that feeling of being needed will begin to overwhelm and consume you. It will chain you like a slave to that feeling. It's not a sustainable state of life to live in. This neediness will only lead to stress, anxiety, and ultimately, defeat.

We desperately long to be useful and have purpose, but we usually settle for needed, not holding out for desired. People often sling around the phrase "We need to be needed." I'm not quite sure that's exactly the case, but I do know it's a pleasant feeling to bring something to the table, especially something that someone needs. The point is that God doesn't need us, he doesn't need me, he doesn't need you, and he doesn't need the church either. God doesn't even need your money. Listen to what David had to say about it:

> Listen, my people, and I will speak;
> I will testify against you, Israel:
> I am God, your God.
> I bring no charges against you concerning your sacrifices
> or concerning your burnt offerings, which are ever before me.
> I have no need of a bull from your stall
> or of goats from your pens,
> for every animal of the forest is mine,
> and the cattle on a thousand hills.
> I know every bird in the mountains,
> and the insects in the fields are mine.

> *If I were hungry I would not tell you,*
> *for the world is mine, and all that is in it.*
> *Do I eat the flesh of bulls*
> *or drink the blood of goats?*[1]

But here's the right hook, the turnaround, the main event:

God doesn't *need* you but he *desperately loves* you.

God wants and desires you more than you've ever felt in this life before. Think about the top moments throughout your life where you sat back and thought this is it, this is what life is about. Take that feeling of belonging and contentment and multiply that by whatever number you want because God's love is abundantly more than that. It's something we've never fully experienced before; we only see small glimpses of it. You see, God doesn't need you—instead, he actively chooses you. You're a first-round draft every season, no matter if you have good stats or not. Simply who you are is enough. That is the heart of God, redeeming prisoners and setting captives free.

From the beginning he knew it would cost him dearly, the giving of his Son, but he counted the cost and he decided you were worth it. There's nothing more to argue about or consider; that's how astounding his love is. Our design and meaning in this lifetime are to enjoy the presence of God and find our ultimate fulfillment through him, then go and do something about it. It's the call for adventure and the invitation to freedom.

When we know the reason we are placed on earth, suddenly things take on a new meaning. The sun breaks forth and

---

[1] Psalm 50:7-13

the fog dissipates, revealing our situation in a whole new light. Don't lose the truth in the simplicity of the matter. We over-complicate and miss things because we make ourselves believe that the truth has to be harder than it is. It's not. This is the truth of our situation: the reason we are alive and breathing at this moment is simply for the fact that God created us just as we are and he absolutely delights in our uniqueness, oddities, personalities, character flaws, and everything else about us. He will even use those flaws to bring glory to himself.

If our primary goal is to exist and bring God glory through enjoyment of community with him and others, then we can effectively huck the weighty baggage we've been carrying off the side of the cliff. This is the entirety of all of life's shortcomings and scars, the weight we've been carrying trying to prove our worth. Our worth doesn't have to be derived from anything else on earth; in fact, we will never fully find our deepest worth while searching for it in the here and now.

This concept frees us to live a life we've always imagined, giving us the choice to pursue the adventure God has placed in front of us. We can elevate God and delight in him and others whether that is snowboarding the Swiss Alps, surfing down the coast of South America, finding the cure for cancer, spending time with our families, watching a sunset, introducing our-selves to a stranger—anything and everything we are capable of doing can be done for the glory of God. There are aspects of God's character and heart in the midst of everyday things. When we choose to open our eyes, we are able to enjoy God more fully in our daily lives. Even the tiniest details in life are reflections of God's perfect plan and redemption of a broken world; they tell the story of who God is. All of life tells God's story.

When I understand the gravity and the impact of this principle, it releases me from the heaviness I've placed on my own shoulders, the restraints I've placed on my own wrists. God doesn't expect all of this out of me. I no longer have to be my own savior. It's taken me a long time to recognize the influence and clarity it brings day after day in my life. I feel the weightlessness and liberty to pursue my dreams and the adventures God continually places in my life.

By nature I'm a doer. I love to accomplish things in life because I find most of my life's meaning in accomplishments. I find excitement in creating things and producing quality results. I think we all do. It's a good thing because it's a reflection of who God is—the Creator. When we create or produce, we reflect him and his character.

What isn't healthy is the fact that I commonly pursue this too far. I start to do it for myself, for my own good and my own glory. I find my worth in my doing and not in God and who God says I am. I go overboard because I'm driven to be important, to be needed, to be the best in order that others will love me, want me, and tell me that I'm important, that I matter. When I experience the purifying love of Jesus, I am able to pursue less and give that need and drive to God—the only one who could ever fulfill on the promise of life. This isn't new to our human nature, but it does reoccur in my life every day when I seek satisfaction and gratification in and of myself and my abilities, spending my labor on what does not satisfy.

This is what Isaiah said over 2,500 years ago:

> *Come, all you who are thirsty,*
> *come to the waters;*
> *and you who have no money,*

> *come, buy and eat!*
> *Come, buy wine and milk*
> *without money and without cost.*
> *Why spend money on what is not bread,*
> *and your labor on what does not satisfy?*
> *Listen, listen to me, and eat what is good,*
> *and you will delight in the richest of fare.*
> *Give ear and come to me;*
> *listen, that you may live.*[2]

Looking through this lens of why we exist and what we are made for brings light and meaning to the entirety of the Bible, providing deeper context to the larger questions in our story. It's the settling of the murky water, sifting and draining what's unnecessary to find what genuinely matters. Perspective changes everything.

Don't take my word for it; take God at his word, always. A great place to start would be in the beginning of our story in the first chapter of Genesis. Regardless of how you feel about creation, I believe the beginning is always the best place to start in order to find out where we belong in the greater context of life. While reading, keep searching for answers to the vital question, "Why would God choose to create mankind when he was perfectly content in and of himself within the Trinity?" God knew that at our best we wouldn't actually produce something he couldn't on his own. It's out of an abundance of his heart that he chooses to give us life, to teach, and to discipline us in order to prove his love to us as his children. Resting in God's character and wholeness is the only time in my life where

---

[2] Isaiah 55:1-3

I feel completely vulnerable and still, at ease. Sitting back and resting in God are some of my greatest memories. No matter what is happening, to be able to stop and meditate on who God is brings peace and calmness that overflow and transcend any situation I find myself in. I can take the weight off and place that on Jesus. I cannot save myself, and God doesn't expect or demand that either. It brings Psalm 23:1-4 to life:

The Lord is my shepherd, I lack nothing.
He makes me lie down in green pastures,
He leads me beside quiet waters,
He refreshes my soul.
He guides me along the right paths
For his name's sake.
Even though I walk
Through the darkest valley,
I will fear no evil,
For you are with me;
Your rod and your staff,
They comfort me.

It's humbling to perceive things as they actually are and not the way we view the world through our warped perspective. This verse is a staple in my life, always bringing my perspective back into the correct context of how trivial we are and how immense God is. What is man that God should care for him?

When I consider your heavens,
The work of your fingers,
The moon and the stars,
Which you have set in place,
What is mankind that you are mindful of them,

Human beings that you care for them?[3]

If you are loved for who you are and not what you produce or contribute, something whimsical happens: you grow to love everything and everyone around you. You no longer have to live a life based solely on your performance. You can fail, and God still loves and accepts you. When you are desired, you start desiring to give, not just take. It's a perpetual journey marked by growth and love, developing into who you've always dreamed of being. Being loved for who you are is truly the greatest security we will ever know. It's the essence of community. Living a life marked by God's radical love naturally leads to peace, refuge, and an incomparable ability to give love away like Jesus. God doesn't need you; but he loves you and calls you his own. It's not just empty words or meaningless phrases; God showed that love for you time after time and is continuing to pour that love over you day after day.

[3] Psalm 8:3-4

3 *IDENTITY CRISIS*

Looking around our culture you'll notice a common denominator: we are all striving for more. We are unsatisfied with who we are, we are unsatisfied with what we have, and we all live under the notion that we deserve more. From the abundance of self-help books to magazines to television programs with 7 quick and easy steps, we are all seeking to squeeze more out of life. We are seeking this validation in all the wrong places.

One of the greatest influences on our character is the people we choose to surround ourselves with. This shouldn't be quite a surprise, but we often overlook the simplicity of this principle. We are attracted to the people who are like us, the people who accept us. It's a security mechanism; we long to belong with like-minded people. Studies have proven numerous times that your five closest friends will have the greatest influence on your life more so than anything else. Your closest group of friends will ultimately steer the direction of your life.

Around us, we see everyone longing to belong—to be the same as others by doing the same things and owning the same stuff. Marketing thrives on our need of belonging and our herd mentality. Everyone is preaching about individuality, yet everyone is doing the exact same thing. We buy the same clothing, we eat the same food, we drive the same cars, we live in the same neighborhoods, we go to the same schools, and we eventually become the same people.

What society isn't telling us is the fact that you don't have to be the same. You have the ability to be different, to be free from the pressures of herd mentality. When you know who you are, only then are you able to set the world on fire with your passions and desires that are unique in you. You don't have to constantly seek approval in others' opinions of your story. You are able to form your own opinion without having to fear the judgment of the crowd. You have the power to change the environment you live in. If we long to be the same as everyone else, we will never make a difference.

While researching identity crises, I came across one of the most widely renowned developmental psychologists and psychoanalysts, known for his theory on psychosocial development, Erik Erikson. Erikson was an ego psychologist. He emphasized the role of culture and society and the conflicts that can take place within the ego itself.

According to sources, "He may be most famous for coining the phrase identity crisis." I had been aware of his psychosocial development theory since we constantly use that in the hospital setting. It's a remarkable tool that adequately depicts life in eight distinct stages from birth to death. Erickson was a highly intelligent individual and what he had to say on identity crises is worth listening to. This is what Erickson had to say:

> They often seem to have no idea who or what they are, where they belong or where they want to go. They may withdraw from normal life, not taking action or acting

as they usually would at work, in their marriage or at school. They may even turn to negative activities, such as crime or drugs, as a way of dealing with identity crisis. To someone having an identity crisis, it is more acceptable to them to have a negative identity than none at all.[1]

Researchers have found that those who have made a strong commitment to an identity tend to be happier and healthier than those who have not. Those with a status of identity diffusion tend to feel out of place in the world and don't pursue a sense of identity. In other words, they're lost.

In today's rapidly changing world, identity crises might be more common than in Erikson's era of the '60s. These conflicts are certainly not confined to the teenage years as some have previously suggested. People tend to experience them at various points throughout life, particularly at points of great change, such as starting a new career, the beginning of a new relationship, the end of a marriage, a new medical diagnosis, or the birth of a child. Exploring different aspects of yourself in the different areas of life, including your role at work, within the family, and in relationships, can help strengthen your personal identity.

It seems as if we struggle through this stage where we are seeking an identity to become more than we currently are. I would argue that it seems to last until we find that identity. Many people never truly discover who they are, why they are here, and consequently never find their purpose. People learn to live in the state of the unknown, without building their lives

---

[1] www.liquisearch.com/identity_crisis/concept

on a solid foundation of identity. In our day and age, it's crucial to understand who we are if we have any desire to change ourselves or the world around us. We can't change anything if we're the same as the environment we live in. It's difference that shapes who we are, that makes us stand apart. Our uniqueness, our talents, and our faults—those are the things that shape and mold us.

Knowing who we are is more than a flashy psychology topic, new blog post or anything else. I strongly believe this is one of the foundations of gaining momentum in your life, shaping your influence to impact the world around you. It's such a rare sight to see someone who stands apart from the crowd and embraces their differences rather than hiding behind walls they have built over time. You will not thrive in life if you don't come to the understanding of who you are as a person.

One of my first nursing professors during my freshman year at university always wore the same baseball cap each week to class. The hat read, "Only bad girls make history." The best part of the story is that she had to be well over 87 years old. I can't remember much from the class and I think the same goes for the other three hundred students who were in the same lecture. It was an easy A, and it was a class that was mandatory to advance in the program.

At the time I didn't know it, but that statement had a huge impact on me. It's the primary thing I learned all semester. It's only the outliers who cause a disruption to the system and spur change. If you're average—and that's not wrong—you'll simply end up just like everyone else. If you're willing to be different and take a risk, then you'll have an abundance of opportunities to change the things you see in the world, to make a clear difference in the lives of people.

To risk being different always comes at a price. It might cost you friends, family, security, comfort, relationships, health, money, or countless other things. These are daily struggles we face. Every choice we make has the ability to set us apart from the culture we live in. It's difficult keeping ourselves accountable, having the discipline of making these hard choices, because we are constantly surrounded by easy alternatives. It seems like no one is keeping track if you take the long way or the shortcut. What you put in now is what you will take out later; what you sow is what you will reap. I cannot tell you how many times this principle has proven true in my life, for the good things and the bad.

Identity crisis is the state of the unknown. It's constantly asking, "Who am I?" Some days we seem to know the answer and other days it seems like the opposite is true. It's a war within us that puts us on edge, living between who we are and who we desire to be. We try to mask the confusion and hide the pain with distraction: anything that will take our minds off the subject, such as busyness, the hustle of the daily grind, TV, sports, pursuing education, career work, or anything to break the silence. The silence reveals the inner workings of our identity issues by bringing them to the surface. It's much easier to suppress those issues by distractions or pleasure.

We hate silence. The silence brings things to the surface that we would rather keep buried in the deep of the unknown rather than dealing with intimate issues. So we avoid the uneasiness by constant distraction, but when we search deep enough within, we'll find that the internal struggle has metastasized into our daily lives. I find this true of myself. I constantly have music playing while at home or driving to the next place. I don't even think about it. I always have something going on in the background of my life keeping me from thinking about the issues that I'm going through. Thinking deeply takes time, effort, and a certain vulnerability that most of the time I'd rather just forget about—filling that void with whatever dirt I can find to shove in the hole.

The question "Who am I?" isn't a bad place to start. Honestly, it's a particularly important question to ask that we should be exploring and trying to map out. When we know who we are, we are able to come alive because we have purpose, passion, and a deeper sense of meaning, and therefore, a deeper satisfaction in life. Simply knowing who you are can change everything. To know who you are and that you belong is a very empowering weapon. You are here in a unique time in history, playing a crucial role only you can play.

But the problem continues because we consistently search for answers in all the wrong places. We're completely missing the mark, and it's killing us from the inside out. We are dying to know who we are. How many times has the phrase "find yourself" been thrown around among our generation? Thousands of times every day we're bombarded with this realization that if we buy specific products and do certain activities, we will find ourselves and life will start to make sense. There is a reason companies spend $180,120,000,000.00 in advertising every year in the United States. One hundred eighty billion dollars on just the chance for you to buy their products. That's a load of money just for a chance that you'll buy it, but advertising continues to climb steadily year after year. We've all heard sex sells when it comes to marketing, and it clearly does. The other thing that sells is the promise of a new life, a meaningful life of abundance and love. Seriously, just buy this new advanced-formula shampoo and your life will never be ordinary again.

We don't believe it, but somewhere deep down we essentially do. It works into our subconscious and formulates who we think we are, or more so, what we think we need to be complete. Marketing has two main goals no matter the product or the service. The first goal is to make you dissatisfied with the way things currently are. The second goal is to fill that void of dissatisfaction with the company's product or the promise of a better life. The reason lifestyle advertisements sell so much, just like sex advertising, is because everyone wants it. We are killing ourselves with boredom; we want to break the mundane. We know deep within we are made for more than working a career for 30-plus years and buying a house to settle down in. We were made for life and when we're bombarded daily with reasons of why we don't add up to the lives of others, it's hard to move forward. Advertising has a crippling effect on us, unless we find our identity and live our lives rooted in the truth. Marketing desires to give you a false identity that lasts only as long as you drive the newest edition of that car, have the newest phone, or the cleanest sneakers. As soon as someone else has something better than you, you no longer hold value as a person, and your identity is lost. The cycle continues, and the only people who win are the companies selling you your false identity.

Maybe you are someone who believes backpacking through Europe will uncover your identity, that you'll find yourself by a wild adventure traveling the globe. Let me tell you something about traversing the globe: your identity isn't overseas. You don't just wake up one day and find yourself in Europe and life instantly makes sense. You simply wake up every day and everyone around you has funny accents. That's what's different. Our identity is not that easy to unmask or everyone would be circumnavigating the globe as we speak. I believe travel is important and will help uncover parts of who you are and what you love about life, but traveling in and of itself will only leave you disappointed if you thought it would bring about a certain clarity about your meaning and purpose. Identity is a deeper issue than a plane ticket or train ride can uncover.

Anyone you meet almost always instinctively asks you, "So what kind of work do you do?" or "What do you do for a living?" Depending on your answer, people make a generalized judgment on your worth, assigning importance to your life. You always know it's coming, and that question never gets easier to answer. It's hard to summarize what we do in one sentence or two. I'm convinced most of the time the person asking doesn't really care what you do. They just want to see if you're somewhat of a threat to them, and if you are, to keep an eye on you in the future.

I used to say it's what you do that actually does defines you. Part of me still believes that, but at the same time I can honestly tell you I've done some messed-up things that were completely out of character for me. That doesn't mean that's who I am. I don't have to let that define me. I strongly believe actions are a much greater indication of who you are than words, but actions still do not necessarily reveal your identity. Your actions do demonstrate a deeper side to who you are, but they don't adequately paint the full picture.

I've done a lot of things; I have a full résumé. I have too many things to put on my résumé. I've done things most people only dream of. It's not enough to satisfy the hunger down inside my soul. During conversations I'll ask people what they want to accomplish with their life or what is their loftiest ambition. I tend to get responses such as to travel through Europe, to build a house, to write a book, to graduate college, to start a business, to run a marathon, and so forth. Those aren't bad dreams, those are great dreams—but I've done those and I can tell you without a doubt that we are made for more than that. I've accomplished all those, and the end of it all is empty. The only thing that runs through my mind is that we were made for so much more than this.

One of our society's favorite lies is the disillusionment of materialism. Materialism is taking over the globe at extreme rates. We all know things don't bring us happiness. We've always kind of known that, but there's a complete disconnect from our heads to our hearts over this issue. Research has found that low self-esteem and materialism are not just a correlation but a causal relationship where low self-esteem increases materialism and active materialism creates low self-esteem. There is a correlation that as self-esteem increases, materialism decreases. Even a simple gesture to raise self-esteem dramatically decreases materialism, which provides a way to cope with insecurity. Materialism is an issue of the heart, an issue stemming from identity crisis.

The problem with materialism and the American dream is the fact that it doesn't fulfill the promise of satisfaction we're desperately searching for in life. It makes a bold statement that it will satisfy us when we make it to the next level in our career, drive a more luxurious car, or live in a bigger house, but in the end we are more stressed, depressed, and empty than when we began chasing after happiness, throwing dollar bills at the issue. "And like the addict, the mindless consumer soon discovers that his high was short-lived and ultimately unsatisfying; furthermore, looking for happiness in all the wrong places has kept him from solving his real problems."[2]

> As Jesus started on his way, a man ran up to him and fell on his knees before him. "Good teacher," he asked, "what must I do to inherit eternal life?" "Why do you call me good?" Jesus answered. "No one is good—except God alone. You know the commandments: 'You shall not murder, you shall not commit adultery, you shall not steal, you shall not give false testimony, you shall not defraud, honor your father and mother.'" "Teacher," he declared, "all these I have kept since I was a boy." Jesus looked at him and loved him. "One thing you lack," he said. "Go, sell everything you have and give to the poor, and you will have treasure in heaven. Then come, follow me." At this the man's face fell. He went away sad, because he had great wealth.[3]

It's easy to let our possessions and titles define our lives. It also makes the world a remarkably shallow place to live. We are compressed down to our résumés and reference letters; those things don't encompass half of who we are. Our society lives only on the surface; there is no depth to people, to business, or to anything. I've accomplished an enormous amount of impactful things in my life and had extreme experiences, but when I look at my résumé I just think to myself, *Is that it? My life is reduced to two pieces of paper?*

---

[2] www.johnplaceonline.com/money_management/19-ugly-things-you-didnt-know-about-materialism/
[3] Mark 10:17-22

Jesus sought out a deeper sense of who we are on the inside. He was able to see past the societal norms and stab straight to the heart of the matter. In the above passage Jesus looked at the wealthy man and loved him. We usually get hung up on the issue of his wealth, and Jesus saw the wealth, saw the success of this man's life, and looked beyond that and loved him. Jesus loves people despite their circumstances. Jesus knew the young man would walk away, yet he loved him anyway. It would be a terrible thing to come to the end of your life only to realize that you walked away from the very Giver of Life in the pursuit of material possessions.

I would like to think we've all been at that point and all tasted what this world can give, leaving an unsatisfactory taste in our mouths. It leaves us longing for more, what we have is never enough, and when we get more; it's still never enough. These empty promises never fulfill us the way we believed they would. One of my favorite quotes is from Jim Carrey when he said, "I think everybody should get rich and famous and do everything they ever dreamed of so they can see that it's not the answer." Jim grew up dirt poor, living out of a van. He ended up rich and famous, living the kind of rags-to-riches story we admire so much. His story is different though; Jim didn't forget his roots or become entangled in the glory of success to lose perspective, and he realized materialism is not all that it seems. He decided to look back and say, it's not everything I dreamed it would be. I need to take these words to heart; I need to actively choose to live my life with that perspective on a daily basis.

Think of the life we could live and the hours we would gain each day by taking the time to realize that the things we commonly pursue in life won't actually solve the issues we have.

What if we stopped chasing after worthless pursuits and started doing things that mattered? What if we invested that time into something that would produce eternal consequences? Our lives are not our own; they were bought at a price. What God has given to us, he will rightfully take back, and with interest.

A fresh perspective changes everything we've known about life in an instant. When we view life this way, everything starts to fall into place and we see why people behave the way they do. Look back over your life at the fights and the divisions over position, over money, over time—it all comes back to a struggle for power. It all comes back to finding our worth in earthly things. We've traded the glory that God desperately desires to paint our lives with for fake satisfaction from earthly things. It doesn't satisfy though, and when we find that out, we are moved to resentment and anger. We start to compare our lives with others. We start to bicker and snarl at one another over meaningless things.

It's a sad reality we live in. We see and hear things like this daily, and yet we have a hard time connecting the fragments together. How often do we hear churches split over a power struggle? All I can think about is what Jesus would have to say on the matter. The very place that shouldn't be tainted, and the one thing that shouldn't matter to us, is destroying all of our relationships. It's not okay to keep acting like this while claiming to be followers of Jesus. Jesus took a completely different approach, and furthermore he was the only one who deserved all the power. In spite of that, he came to seek and save that which was lost. He gave power away in order to have relationships with the least of these. In contrast to Jesus, we give relationships away in order to gain power. We're destroying everything Jesus came to teach us.

One of my favorite passages is found in Philippians 2. This is what it has to say on the subject.

Therefore if you have any encouragement from being united with Christ, if any comfort from his love, if any common sharing in the Spirit, if any tenderness and compassion, then make my joy complete by being like-minded, having the same love, being one in spirit and of one mind. Do nothing out of selfish ambition or vain conceit. Rather, in humility value others above yourselves, not looking to your own interests but each of you to the interests of the others.
In your relationships with one another, have the same mindset as Christ Jesus:
Who, being in very nature God,
did not consider equality with God something to be used to his own advantage;
rather, he made himself nothing
by taking the very nature of a servant,
being made in human likeness.
And being found in appearance as a man,
he humbled himself
by becoming obedient to death—
even death on a cross!
Therefore God exalted him to the highest place
and gave him the name that is above every name,
that at the name of Jesus every knee should bow,
in heaven and on earth and under the earth,
and every tongue acknowledge that Jesus Christ is Lord,
to the glory of God the Father.

When we know who we are, we are then free to become anything we've ever dreamed of. We don't have to live for the approval of others. We can live unashamed of our past, uncovering the scars and the character flaws, and become vulnerable because Jesus tells us who we are. Jesus tells us that we are pure, forgiven, and loved.

It's hard to live this out in a broken world where we are repeatedly told we are mistakes, a random chance by an explosion, evolved from pasty mud, have no value in life, and we have no real beauty or larger story to be a part of. We suppress into an average life because the power of Satan keeps us from realizing our new identity in Jesus Christ. What God has to say on the matter of identity is critical to all aspects of life. It will always be a struggle to decide whose voice you will listen to. Some days Satan wins my attention while Jesus has the words of life. I choose to listen to the voice telling me I'm worthless, that my past is too broken, and that I can't influence others because of the mistakes I've repeatedly made. I spent too many days and nights listening to the voice in the darkness, all the while Jesus was telling me I was made new, given life through his sacrifice, that I was loved more than I could imagine, and seen as perfect through his eyes.

Every day I need to choose to take Jesus at his word, to live out what Jesus has spoken into my life with authenticity and courage that come from believing that Jesus' words are true. I need the daily reminder that God's heart is good and loving toward me with the power and authority to back it up. His actions are directly in line with his words.

People are waiting for someone to come along who is fully alive, rooted in their identity, someone of substance. They're dying for it actually. We are so unsure of ourselves when we try to define who we are by our occupations, hobbies, possessions, body type, or relationships. And probably for good reason, because we've made some serious mistakes and can still feel the pain and the deep hurt within who we are when we try to derive our identity from these broken sources of life. This pain is way deeper than physical pain; this is a kind of spiritual pain related to separation from the direct source of love we've been created to receive. We've longed for this sense of completeness since the beginning.

When I find that completeness in my identity through God, I don't have to find it in anything else. I am set free. I am no longer a slave to society and the broken demands it confines me to. I no longer have to save myself or die trying. Jesus already did that.

I don't want to be that guy who says, "Hey man, just give it to God. God is the answer to everything. Life is perfect—just let go and let God." I don't want to be that guy. But clearly we need an outside validation of our lives and our stories to tell us that we are enough, that we are valued, and that we are loved. From experience, I know I've felt that validation from God time after time—the kind where I experience true peace. The peace where I could be wrong and still smile. It is the kind of peace when I was cheated out of money, I could still be positive. The kind of peace where everything falls apart, but I know life is beautiful. The peace that says with God this is possible. I don't need any validation from this world, material things, mobs of people, or social media because when it comes from God, and only from God, it fulfills something inside of me that I've been desperately craving my entire life.

Do I still long for your approval? More than you could imagine. Do I love it when people speak into my life and tell me I made a difference? More than you could imagine. The problem exists when I choose to find my satisfaction and approval for my life in people's praises of what I've accomplished, instead of finding my worth and value in who God tells me I am. It's easy to find that meaning in other people; it's what we've been groomed to do our entire lives. Society is built on this principle, but it will always leave us thirsty for something more.

Can you imagine life if you didn't need validation from other people, work, relationships, your parents, or your own ambitions? I'll tell you what it would look like: it would look a lot like Jesus. It would be radical. How different would we live if we sought complete validation from God instead of from our current circumstances?

I'd say, it's worth thinking about. God changed my life and validated my story. I felt the need to validate my life from others, my parents, my brother, and even myself. Learning to let go of those heavily weighted expectations of gaining validation from those sources and seeking my value from the one true source of life has drastically changed my perspective. Only God can give me what I truly desire; it's time for me to let him.

I've come to find that God isn't the one who usually yells over the noise. God patiently waits for us to be silent in order to fill us with what we need. God is longing to paint the picture of who we are; we simply have to be still enough to be the canvas. The more I find who I am in Jesus, the more I find who I was created to be.

Take, for example, a man named Gary—the man who lives the dream. He sleeps around with whoever he wants—the most beautiful women Miami has to offer. Drinks what he wants, tallying up a bill that is comparable to three times my monthly rent plus utilities. He also travels wherever he wants, and buys whatever car he wants when he wants it. He lives in one of the most expensive condos on the planet. Famous celebrities seek him out for his expertise. Everything he desires he has. He's almost comparable to a modern-day Solomon. He has it all. He has everything a man could dream of.

Except for love.

Unfortunately, he gave up on love years ago.

Don't get me wrong, He was an incredible host and I had a remarkable time cruising around Miami with him and my friend Luke, but you could tell something was missing in his life. He toured us through the real Little Havana, showing us all the culture and hidden gems along the way that ordinary people would never know existed. He took us to a famous diner and generously footed the bill for everyone. He was flashy, but he had reason to be.

He's everything the modern man desires to become. Money, cars, girls—whatever you want he's already got it. All that society tells us that should fulfill and sustain us, Gary has that. All the earthly success and power one could desire, he's got that.

What he has is everything we as a society have deemed important and life-giving. We are deceived that these things will bring validation and a new identity to who we are. But we continue chasing these empty pursuits because we believe it will be different for us. It will be different when I get these things. We wouldn't be like other famous people or celebrities. When we make it, we'll be happy, we'll be complete, and it will be enough for us.

But he's broken. He's empty. Everything else in his life

seems like it fell apart a long time ago. Those girls, those cars, that power don't seem that important without a loving family, or a real community to celebrate your successes with. Honestly, without love everything else is meaningless. He has all these things, yet he is empty. He traded them for success and for fame. A long time ago he sold his character to become something better in the eyes of the world. He sold out, and his integrity washed along with it.

The story continues after the fact my friend Luke spent three months working for this guy's firm in Miami. It was a wild work environment to say the least. Drugs, alcohol, and big money are just a small part of the everyday happenings that surrounded Luke. VIP placement in the hottest nightclubs in the world, and bosses casually doing lines of cocaine with the interns were the norm. That's to put the story into perspective of Miami and the work environment Luke found himself in. It's rough and wild, and more extreme than most internships.

But when I heard the boss telling my friend Luke, after his three month internship, that what he valued and respected most about Luke is the simple fact he knows exactly who he is and what he stands for, I was so proud. He's solid. He knows his identity. What a testimony of my friend Luke. I was blown away.

My best friend was offered the best of the world and peered into all of it and decided to stand for more—to stand for love, hope and redemption—actual life, authentic life, not a small counterfeit for the real thing. Luke didn't sell out. Luke stood for what he believed in. Luke knew his identity.

"You stand out because you know who you are. I respect

that," Gary told my friend Luke. "You realize that this world needs you and everything else is just details." Luke didn't get distracted; he didn't lose his mission; he didn't compromise who he was in order to fit in down in Miami.

God has placed a calling in your life, to give you a new identity in him. He created you to be in perfect unity in stride with himself, walking side by side through this life together. We traded that offer a long time ago for a lie of something better. God, out of his goodness and love, has extended that offer to each one of us—the offer for a new identity, to be made new, to be made pure once again. Through the blood of Jesus, we are cleansed and made holy in the eyes of God our Father. There's no dirt that won't wash away in the blood of Jesus. We are made new. Our identity is no longer found in the broken and empty lies of society—it is found in being called a child of God.

When we grasp that concept, this world will be shaken at the core.

Life starts to come into focus when we take the emphasis off ourselves and place it on Jesus. We can only do this when we let God tell us who we are. I believe the key to living a dangerous life that matters for eternity is coming to the end of yourself, and letting God dictate the chapters to your story. The best place to find yourself is where you lose yourself in the workflow of what God is doing in the world. When we realize life isn't about us, that's when things start coming alive.

4 *PROVING GROUNDS*

Validation is one of the major driving factors in all of life, perhaps the main driving factor in life. When you keep your eyes open and study how people live, digging into human behavior, you'll find that people are actively seeking validation from something or someone. People are waiting for something or someone to come along and validate their situation. We're waiting for someone to tell us that we matter, that we have worth, that what we do is purposeful, and that we aren't wasting our lives.

We crave, desperately crave, validation.
That's why guys sleep with girls.
That's why girls sleep with guys.
That's why we have to prove ourselves.
That's why we always have to be right.
That's why we always have to have the final word.
That's why we can't take responsibility.
That's why we can't apologize.
That's why we give into peer pressure.
That's why we jump from relationship to relationship.

We are creatures who crave validation from anything we think will satisfy, even when we understand that it won't last. We desire to feel important, special, and loved. We were made for validation we just haven't found it yet.

We seek validation in everything. We desire to know we have what it takes. We want to know that we are good enough. But the world can't tell you that. Drinking a case of beer won't tell you that you're a man. Sleeping with a different girl each week won't validate your life. Driving a brand-new corvette can't tell you that. The magnitude only grows, but the feeling never leaves. We can't find validation, the validation we need, from material things.

Maybe you realize that we can't find it in material possessions, but maybe you're holding out to find it in another person, to find validation in love. Reasonable, right?

But we won't find it in another person. That's why so many marriages fail. They can't give you that validation and you shouldn't expect them to either. We place this undue burden on our partner—a burden they were never made to carry. Maybe they can show you a deeper side and bring out quality traits in you, but you can't ask them to validate your life. No matter who he or she is, they will never be enough to fill you. They weren't designed to.

Someone once told me a simple analogy that explained our human power struggle in a concept that I would be able to translate into any situation. He called it the boat theory. This theory altered my life. It made sense of all the experiences I could think back upon and brought clarity to all the fights, divisions, and frustrations I could remember that marked my past.

The boat theory is essentially the struggle of five people fighting over the position in a four-person safety raft. Since there is only enough room for four people to survive, everyone is fighting for the approval of the others on the raft in order to stay alive. Someone is going to get thrown to the sharks, and everyone is struggling to make sure it's not them. To stay alive you have to prove your worth to the others in the boat, convincing them you possess worth to the group and are a better person than the others who are also trying to convince the group of their own worth. While others are trying to convince or deceive the group of their identity and worth, they are constantly tearing each other down in order to make themselves look more appealing, more like the one who belongs, the one to survive.

One person might be pregnant; one person might be rich; one person might be a CEO; one person might be homeless, and one person might be the average Joe, but you have to decide who stays in the life raft and who gets tossed to the sharks. One person isn't going to make it out alive, and it's in our fate to decide who is worthy or not.

The five people in the life raft are desperately doing whatever it takes to prove their value to one another. We live our lives the same way. We don't think of it as life-or-death situations, but we do whatever it takes to prove to others we have it all together, that we have value, that we are exactly what people need. We are begging to stay afloat on the raft.

We live our lives trying to convince each other of our worth. We spend so much energy, money, and stress to prove ourselves to others. That's why we take things so personally. That's why it's hard to laugh at ourselves. That's why we're a society so afraid of mistakes. We've been groomed to believe we have to have it all together or else we don't matter; we don't have value.

It doesn't matter if you were one of the four who actually stayed on the raft. Your life is going to come to a close. Your position or your self-imposed importance may gain you influence and a good life, but in the light of eternity it means nothing. We're destroying opportunities to love others because we're fighting over our own importance and pride. Our worth shouldn't come from man's validation of us. That only ends in brokenness and pain. Our validation should come from God telling us that we are enough, that we are indeed loved and delighted in, that we are designed with meaning and purpose, that our stories matter.

What we miss out on during the entire proving "we're the best" phase is actual life. We forfeit our lives, our identities, and who we are to prove to other people that we're good enough. The problem is the fact that even when other people agree that we are good enough, that isn't enough to validate our situations. We're still empty and searching for a deeper meaning, even though we spent years grinding away to achieve other peoples' validation. It won't ever be enough.

When we are able to separate ourselves and step back from the cyclical validation structure, we are able then to pursue something bigger with our lives, something that matters. We are in a constant battle of choosing which voice we will listen to—the voice of the world or the voice of the one who conquered the world and put death in its place. It's a hard fight that will continually drain you mentally, physically and spiritually, but it will also be the battle that sets you apart from the rest of the world. The voice we listen to will dictate how our thoughts, words and eventually actions are formed and how these slowly cultivate into who we become. Our core is being transformed by the thousands of small choices we make on a daily basis.

Once in a while we encounter someone who charges after life with unparalleled boldness, someone who is alive at their core. It's those people who inspire me to bring the best out of myself. They have qualities and characteristics that I never will possess, but they instantly make you better. You desire to live life the way they do. They're comfortable in their own skin; they love the life they live, and they're proud of who they are. They're not proud in an arrogant way, but they have a genuineness to their character.

Of all these people that I've encountered in my own life— these people who I desire to become, to mold my life after—all of them come upon defeat, crippling times, and isolation. The difference is that they were willing to look beyond the here and now, peer beyond man's validation and seek the approval of God. They took God at his word and chose to become part of the solution. They chose responsibility. They decided to act on the promises of God. They aren't perfect, and they'll be the first to tell you that, but they believed God was able to use them to impact those around them despite their brokenness.

It would be a devastating waste if you hid the deepest parts of yourself from the world, in a false sense of security. The world desperately needs you in such a time as this. People need others who are willing to be authentic and those who are willing to be flawed, scarred, and messed up. God accepts you with all your flaws and insecurities. Not only does he accept you with all your flaws and imperfections, he loves you that way. The very things we consider unredeemable qualities in ourselves are exactly what God uses to bring out his own glory in our lives. It's in those weaknesses that Paul was able to boast:

> *But he said to me, "My grace is sufficient for you, for my power is made perfect in weakness." Therefore I will boast all the more gladly about my weaknesses, so that Christ's power may rest on me. That is why, for Christ's sake, I delight in weaknesses, in insults, in hardships, in persecutions, in difficulties. For when I am weak, then I am strong.*[1]

I know finding your identity will change your life because it completely changed mine. I don't have to walk around trying to prove that I'm good enough anymore. I did that long enough. I needed to prove to everyone including myself, predominantly myself, that I was good enough—that I mattered, that I had purpose, and that I could make it. Growing up, I never felt adequate. I never felt like I was good enough for my family, for my friends, and definitely not for God. I became a producer, a doer, someone of action so that if I wasn't enough, at least people would want me for what I could accomplish.

It was so hard to go through most of life not fully feeling my parents love for me. The love they continually poured over me never seemed like enough, and I still felt like I was inadequate, like I didn't belong in my own family. It ripped me apart. They had given me everything I had ever needed, the best love parents could ever provide, and yet somehow I was blind to that love most of my life. I felt inadequate and not good enough for my parents' love for me. I didn't know who I was. I struggled to find value in life. I was broken, hopeless, and aimlessly searching for something of substance.

---

[1] 2 Corinthians 12:9-11

Now I know who I am and what I stand for. I am able to freely accept the love that has been poured out for me. I don't have to walk around seeking the approval of others, buying the lies society is selling. I can be free and vulnerable. I don't have to protect or project an image of who I am anymore. I can let the weight fall at the foot of the cross. My past no longer has a grip on my life, because Jesus has ripped it off and thrown it into the depths of the sea. Now I can be open about my mistakes and failures with others. I don't need society's stamp of approval when I have the approval of Jesus, declaring over my life that I am loved and that I am enough.

It's not only that I'm good enough, because I'm not. It's the fact that Jesus took my place of condemnation and traded his crown and righteousness with my own brokenness and shame. I am no longer trapped by a false identity. I have been set free. I have been made new. I am no longer defined by my dirty past. I am defined by the righteousness found in Jesus. He has validated my situation and spoken life into my story.

I didn't know who I was until God told me who I was by speaking into my wounds. He brought me through numerous painful experiences that have shaped me into the man I am today. Every transformation in life is painful. We don't cope well with change. When that change is the core of who we are, it will certainly be a painful experience. God places people in our lives at unique times to tell us and to point us to who we are and who we can become. It could be that stranger or a friend encouraging you to try something new, or to continue pursuing your dreams, or simply telling you that you're good at something. Countless times I've doubted my abilities, only to be reaffirmed that day or the next about something I did that made a lasting impact. Even something I doubted the whole time created a powerful impact because I knew that I was unable to accomplish this feat alone.

I think Satan makes you doubt what you're supposed to do in order to induce fear to keep you from what the Lord is actively doing. God challenges it in the exact opposite way by affirming your gifts. He doesn't take the fear or risk away; he simply reaffirms your mission and says, "Watch me." It's not easy to pick one voice over the other, but the choice is always ours to make. I pray we all start acting on the right voice. The best times of my life are the ones where I've chosen to listen to that inner voice and decided to live it out instead of passing up the opportunity due to my own fear or inadequacy.

I've missed moments where I felt God's leading in my life because I thought the risk was too much, the danger too high, so I let my fear hold me back. Did God still accomplish his mission? Yeah, I think so. But at the same time God, in his loving discipline, was wishing I had trusted him in order to gain the experience he had planned for me all along. I decided from those moments onward that whenever I felt that nudging that I would take the leap of faith no matter what the cost. I'm tired of letting fear dictate the outcome of my life. God is bigger than any fear that I will ever have.

Therefore, if anyone is in Christ, the new creation has come: The old has gone, the new is here! All this is from God, who reconciled us to himself through Christ and gave us the ministry of reconciliation: that God was reconciling the world to himself in Christ, not counting people's sins against them. And he has committed to us the message of reconciliation. We are therefore Christ's ambassadors, as though God were making his appeal through us. We implore you on Christ's behalf: Be reconciled to

God. God made him who had no sin to be sin for us, so that in him we might become the righteousness of God.[2]

We have a radical opportunity to be different, to be set apart, for a wholesome purpose by taking what God has spoken into our lives and using that for his benefit and glory. It seems upside down to live with our hearts on our sleeves while boasting in our weaknesses, but that is exactly what God is asking of us. Without risk there is no return. Don't walk around hiding your flaws and covering up your mistakes. We're not called to be perfect; we're called to be desperately reliant on God and his never-ending grace. When we chase perfection instead of grace, we become reliant on ourselves and not on God. What made the disciples great wasn't their talents, raw abilities, or knowledge; it was that they took Jesus at his word and lived that out.

This world needs you—not who society defines you as, but who God created you to be. Let him speak freely into your life. Explore your passions and pursue them with every ounce of energy inside of you. Give all of yourself away to others; die empty. You have unique gifts and talents that I don't possess; only you can reach certain people groups that need to know the story of redemption in ways no one will ever be able to convey besides you. Do everything in your power to become the person God is asking you to be. You will never regret for a second a life lived on God's terms.

One of the sad things about our culture is the inability to show weakness. We think we have to constantly have every-

---

[2] 2 Corinthians 5:17-21

thing together or we won't be accepted. We walk around with perfectly painted faces, pretending we have all the answers. We disillusion each other to think we're exactly where we want to be in life. The truth is, we're all seeking validation and meaning in our lives. We think maybe when we hit age 25 or graduate with a master's degree, we'll know what we're supposed to do, but I keep meeting people in their 50s and 60s still looking for their purpose in life.

It's no different inside the walls of the church. Church seems to be a place you go and everything is "good." The week was hell, but as soon as we burst through those doors, then man, life is good. That slightly odd guy holding open the door Sunday mornings with the cheesiest smile he can condjure yells across the parking lot, "Hey budddddddy, how's it going?" Instantly, you respond with the classic line of "good" without even thinking twice. Then the coffee lady asks how things are and you instantly respond, "Good. Everything is great. You?"

Well, maybe everything is good and everything in your life is great. Mine isn't. It feels like one day I'm on top of Mt. Everest and the next few hundred days I'm struggling through the desert, dehydrated, with a sandstorm blowing straight in my eyes. My skin is burning, my camel died years ago, the only thing I've eaten for weeks is sand, and I don't even have aviator sunglasses or one of those cool desert scarf things like in the movies. That's how I feel most days, walking around the desert trying not to die.

It's impossible to grow and develop into the man or woman God is calling you to become if we cannot be honest with God, honest with each other, and honest with ourselves. The good news is that God already knows you inside and out—the good, the bad, the doubts, the insecurities—and loves you the same. Façades are keeping us from a deeper sense of meaning and purpose we all desire in life. You will never find what you're looking for until you stop pretending with God and yourself.

You already know your doubts and insecurities, but it'll take some digging to get to the bottom of it all—the real substance—because we've buried those doubts and wounds years ago in the subconscious of our minds. It will be painful to dig deep and pull those repulsive memories and painful experiences out into the open. It's also the only way we will ever find true healing. The hard part about that is opening yourself—your scars, your wounds, your doubts, and your insecurities—entirely in order for you to pursue God in a deeper context. You don't have to fight this battle alone. You don't have to wage war without an ally. God can and will bring healing when we place our insecurities at his feet. He will show us the true depth of our longing and fill every void that has been left in our lives from the scars and the pain. He longs to wholly love you and embrace you unconditionally. We only have to open up and let him. God cannot do so fully when we are still holding onto our baggage. We have to let go of our own chains and run into the Father's outstretched arms.

We need to be able to freely ask and explore in a deeper context some of the doubts we have about God and his nature. Some of the biggest doubts I have are these: Can God actually love me? Can God love someone like me? After all the times I've struggled and failed, can God really want someone so dirty, broken, jacked up and worthless?

I became the exception to the rule. I didn't believe God saw anything of value inside of me. How could he when all I seemed to do was destructive to him, to people around me, and to myself? My real doubt was in the saving power of Jesus. It's always a deeper issue buried under years and years of masks than what people see on the surface. The question that would keep me up night after night was *"Do I believe that Jesus' sacrifice was enough?"*

And since I didn't, I worked my way, or so I thought I was working my way, into grace. I knew I couldn't; I knew I couldn't earn my way back into a righteous standing before God, but I had to do something, so I worked. I worked hard. Deep within I was completely aware of my deprivation and that I wouldn't ever be able to pave the way for myself. False hope kept the possibility alive that the combination of my work and Jesus' grace would be enough. Life drives you to a dark place when you're trying to earn enough grace to wash yourself pure.

All of my doubt and insecurity carried me to a dark place. It broke me until I couldn't move anymore. I had done everything. I don't say that lightly. I worked until I couldn't work anymore. I found at the end of myself that I wasn't enough. What I found was that validation from any source other than God was empty. I worked for all the world had, and it wasn't enough to satisfy. What I found was that

JESUS + NOTHING = EVERYTHING

I had everything the world had to offer and all I found was brokenness. You don't have to look hard to find that. I thought my situation would be different, that I could be the exception to the rule. I thought my story would have a different ending, that I would find satisfaction in my life pursuits. I thought I would be satisfied. I was wrong. Those empty things could never satisfy the longing of my heart and the deepness of my being.

It's only when I came to the end of myself, to the realization that only Jesus Christ could satisfy the endless hunger within me, that my life drastically changed. That realization made all the difference.

When I saw God in the correct context, everything turned around. I began to live life with purpose and meaning since I knew and was known by the Creator of the universe. Think about that. The same God who created life with a word, designed DNA, that God is the same God who willingly sacrificed himself to save us. He's on our team. He's the captain and you're his first-round pick.

It's hard to fathom the magnitude of God actually desiring us. Nobody has ever really wanted us, not for us, not for long. We're wanted for what we can provide. That may mean different things to each of us, such as security we provide, useful skills, an adventure companion, someone to break the loneliness, but not simply just for who we are. No one ever really goes out of their way to go the extra mile for me. I'm no one important, and I wouldn't expect people to give me their seat or let me go in front of them in line. I wouldn't expect that; I wouldn't want that. But the God of everything, and I mean everything, gave it all up just for the chance of knowing me and having a flourishing relationship with me. God didn't do it because he needs me. He doesn't. God did it all for the relationship and community we would share together. If that doesn't validate your situation in life, absolutely nothing will.

When we stop seeking validation from people and possessions, we will be free to find the validation we've always been searching for in God alone. In turn, that will properly place people and possessions in the correct context for us to use our passions, possessions, and abilities in order to love people. Everything changes when our story is validated by the One who wrote it.

5 THE HEART OF GOD

I often wonder how much we fight, we disagree, and we divide ourselves over an idea or concept we've had wrong since the commencement of that thought in our minds. A lot of people have a misunderstanding of who God is and what his story is about. This misinterpretation plays a vital part in our lives, rendering us ineffective and fearful. It's tragic, and yet that's the case for most of us. That's my story at least.

If I could only grasp a better view of God's heart, I know my world would instantly change. I've seen the power of God played out in the lives of people I know, and it's radical. It's like nothing I've ever experienced before. God's heart is a consuming fire. When you experience the heart of God in action, you can't help but desire more of God. You can't help but give all of yourself away in the pursuit to see God more clearly. That only happens when we're able to keep our eyes open long enough to catch an accurate glimpse of who God is.

Many of us are lost in the facts, figures, and bullet points about God. It's not that he isn't those things; he is, but God is so much more than a list of characteristics and bullet points. Our problem is with the relationship part of the relationship.

It's not much of a relationship with someone if we never take time to get to know who they are. We may know facts about a person and what they like or dislike, but that isn't much to base a relationship on. To know someone intimately as a person, we have to be vulnerable enough to share our desires, wounds, scars, heartbreaks, and the deep longings that make us who we are. Facts and figures only go so far before the relationship goes stale. Without vulnerability, intimacy, and quality time spent together, any relationship will fall apart. There's no intimacy or power behind a relationship that we keep on the surface level; that's simply an acquaintance. No quality relationships casually happen. Quality relationships take intentionality to build.

Furthermore, it doesn't matter if we have a relationship with God if we have the wrong view of God to start with. When we create the god we want to believe in, we miss out on the authentic relationship with the one true God. We've created our own god to fit into our needy schedules and busy lives, and we've lost sight of the God that's evident in the Bible. Have you read those stories? The stories found in the Bible are radical. What God accomplishes is insane. The power of God is unmatched. God is so much more than our American-dream mentality and the prosperity gospel. He's strikingly bigger than that.

We're just fooling ourselves and wasting our time if we believe anything except what is found in Scripture and made known in believers' lives by the Holy Spirit. We started listening more closely to modern-day scientists, good speakers, halfhearted believers and not the actual Bible itself. We are more apt to read the newest bestseller on spirituality than to pick up the very words of Jesus. Maybe that's why we don't see the power of God as strongly or as clearly as we do in the Bible. We've been placing our hope and faith in the god of our

Western society. It's a far stretch from the God we clearly see evident in the Bible.

Someone recently asked what the most critical thing we as followers of Jesus are missing out on. I believe the single most critical aspect we are missing out on is that we are not personally spending quality time growing in knowledge and understanding through the words God has given to us. If this is his heart, his story for us, I think we need to give it more of our time and attention. The writings found in Scripture all are relevant to our modern-day situations. Life flows from our thoughts about God, about life, about meaning, and about purpose. All of these are connected back to the fundamentals surrounding God and how we live out what we believe. Everything is interconnected.

It's interesting anytime the subject of God is brought up in public. You honestly never know what is about to unfold; anything could happen. Of the many times I've overheard or talked with people who are debating God, people usually move toward crude, cold remarks of how terrible God is, that it's all a hoax to indoctrinate our children to live lives of conformity, that you're an uneducated person if you place your faith in God, or that you only believe because you were raised in church. It's nothing new to our generation, though I do believe we are more outspoken about it, bolder in the approach due to our ignorance on social media in all kinds of forms ranging from politics to religion to education and everything in between. God just happens to fit into one of the social highlights that we use to label each other. This has become another way we identify ourselves and line everyone up in order to decide who is a better choice to stay in the lifeboat.

We tend to find our answers in what other people have to say and their opinions on various matters. It's not a terrible thing, but it's all too easy to distort information from truth to hearsay. I cannot tell you how many times I've heard things through others being repeated time after time while the information passed along is incorrect the whole time, even though they claimed it's science or the latest research data. Mistakes happen. Information passed through people is often distorted in part or in whole. Christians are no exception; I am no exception. We hear something moving on a Sunday morning or through a book, and it opens our eyes and teaches us something new and exciting, maybe revealing a different side of God or what he's about and what he's actively doing in the world around us. Without caution we can spread that around and distort things very easily out of context.

We need to lay the solid foundation through Scripture to see who God actually is and his heart. Each source has its place in our lives in their own way; sometimes it takes someone's opinion and experiences to open our eyes to bring a characteristic of God to new light. Look to the source of life; dig deep for the roots and not just the latest blog post. To root ourselves in the gospel daily, we need to go deeper into the text of the Bible, to take those stories and apply those principles to our everyday lives.

There's an absurd amount of terrible Christian writings floating around our generation. I would read an article or a blog post and say, "This is ridiculous. It's backward and setting up my generation for failure while claiming to be more spiritual or live more like Jesus." Then I'd see my friends sharing the posts and the thousands of likes and comments and I couldn't believe it. This isn't who God is; he's bigger than finding a close parking spot at the mall so that we can waste our money on worthless possessions. He's bigger than helping us lose a few pounds around our waistline. God is bigger than our next promotion at work. It's not that God can't do those things; he can with ease, but we've stopped seeing the ultimate power of who God is by limiting him to only the small, insignificant parts of our lives. I'm tired of subpar writings telling us who God is. God is bigger than that. God deserves more than that.

The issue with defining God is that we have a limit to our understanding by the language we speak. We think in words. All we know is formed from the language we speak. You only know what you know because of the words used to describe the science and the matter around you. As a culture we give things names with words, then use those words to shape how we see the world. Each language may use a different word to describe the same thing, but in other languages people may see the exact same object very differently because of the word chosen to represent it.

That's one of the many reasons I'm intrigued by writing. As a writer you can process the ideas and information along with life experiences, typing the exact words onto a blank piece of paper, and then the reader comes along and is able to comprehend what has been written. If the author is clear enough with precise wording, the reader can know exactly what is going on in the author's mind. It can be one of the most vulnerable and exhilarating things to connect with someone over a few words methodically put together.

Problems occur when the two don't sync together. If the author is incomprehensible, it doesn't matter how much time we spend reading; we won't understand. If the author writes in a language the reader doesn't know, it won't benefit the reader at all. It's only when the two are aligned in unity that the message is presented clearly and interpreted accurately by the recipient.

Most days the language between God and what our society has deemed valuable doesn't align. We describe God in English terminology with words like *loving, powerful, good, faithful,* and *gracious,* along with hundreds of other terms. It's not that he isn't these things; it's just that he is boundless and so much more than average descriptions and the depth of these words. We use these words to describe basic everyday things; therefore, the words lose their ultimate value. We cannot adequately describe God using the English language or any language for that matter. Without the correct word, we cannot even begin to move beyond our basic understanding since we are limited to our own crutch of English terminology. God is speaking an entirely different language than we are. We try to translate, but we fall short most of the time.

I believe that's why experiences in nature and through adventure are overwhelmingly powerful. God speaks to our souls through creation using a language not heard, only felt. Many adventures or experiences I've had cannot adequately be put into words. People always ask and the only word that comes to mind is "good." It wasn't good; it was exceptional; it was life altering. But how can I translate to someone who hasn't experienced what hopping on the back of a motorcycle and cruising the dirt roads of Africa or what jumping in a slammed van with fifteen Tanzanians while speaking broken Swahili is like? If we cannot describe our adventure out west snowboarding in Colorado, our surf trip down the California coastline, or our surgical trip to Nicaragua, we're kidding ourselves if we think we can describe God using those same terms.

I realize that I could give you bullet points and verses giving descriptions of God and who he is and what he's done, but I don't think this would help you truly learn more about God. Lists lose the power of capturing the heart and essence of who God is. Facts are head knowledge, and while helpful, they won't really change anything unless applied. We learn about God by doing, by being aware, by looking for his hands and feet moving around us. We don't learn by memorizing a list of bullet points. If you desire to learn more about who God is, you need to open up Scripture for yourself and start devouring it. God is a God of redemption through story. He takes what is broken and completely transforms it into something beautiful, meaningful, and full of life. He is not one to use formulas. He writes new stories, stories of redemption and freedom.

It's one thing to see a list of characteristics and somehow envision what it would look like, but it's a completely different story when we actively participate and see God in action. I think the best way of seeing who God is and where he is on the move is to start running after where God is already working. It's hard to gain momentum when we continue to stand still.

We don't need more lists. We don't need more formulas. There have been plenty of lists of the characteristics of who God is and what he has accomplished, but for me I found I experience God in a deeper context in a community of believers who are living out what they believe. I learned recently that God shows me himself by revealing traits of who he is in the people around me. Whether it was in the complete forgiveness when I cut down a friend, the humble service of someone I respect, the love of a father when he tells me he'll do whatever it takes to get his daughter out of the hospital and be healthy again, the laughter of good company where I cannot smile anymore because of the pain in my facial muscles. Those are the types of moments when I learn who God is. God reveals himself to us through others.

God invites us along on the journey by simply saying, "Come, and you will see." Most of the time we don't have any idea of where God is leading us in the present moments of life. We love to have things planned and the adventure mapped out with the final destination in mind. We like to be prepared. Being prepared saves lives. But following after the heart of God is no safe matter. It is a dangerous and unsafe place to be. You have to continuously be willing to be uncomfortable with the places God is going to take you if you desire to follow and know him more fully.

Go through experiences knowing you'll be changed in the process. Relationships are forged in the fire. The deepest community I've ever been a part of has come from experiences I wasn't sure we'd make it out of alive. It wasn't a team-building exercise; it was trusting each other with our lives. In relationships, our hearts show through our actions.

Things we know:

God knows all.
God always does the right thing.

God is holy. He is set apart. He isn't exactly like us. He's not just a better man. He is God. His heart is to show love and invite us into a deeper community with himself. That's what he desires. That's why God created man. This is where our identity and purpose are found. God is overwhelmingly loving. He is always just, never wrong, all powerful, self-sufficient. He doesn't need. God is all we've ever hoped for or desired in life. Those are fragments of his image. God wants to know you, to love you, and to bring you home as his own. He's not unjust. He's not cruel; he is a father who is desperately craving your love and affection and he's crazy in love with you. There's always room at his table.

The heart of God is the father of the fatherless, the protector of the weak, and strength to the weary. Compassion over condemnation. Love over hate. "How long have I longed to gather you up?" If we didn't know the heart of God and his gracious and loving nature, it wouldn't really matter what he said or did because we wouldn't comprehend the depth without knowing his motives behind it. God's heart is love. God's heart is community. He is an includer. He seeks people out. He invites others to join. He doesn't discriminate against color, race, sex, age, ability, looks, intelligence or language—God desires all. His heart is bigger. His heart is pure. There is no ulterior motive. God loves all. He longs to welcome you home.

When we see the real heart of God, we are more able to fully live our lives for his glory because we know his heart is good. The heart of God is for all people. It's not exclusive; it's inclusive. God doesn't use calculated formulas. God uses stories. God writes stories. These stories are of redemption, of saving his people from bondage. They are stories of sweet victory and triumph over darkness. He pulls us out slowly toward himself in a slow, redeeming process. Step after step he reveals his goodness and faithfulness, proving himself day after day that he is indeed all he says he is.

God is the artist, and we are simply his workmanship. Have you ever created something and were so blown away by the result? There is life that comes from creating something beautiful. You desire to show it off; you desire others to love it and find life from it. We are that special piece of art to God. Out of all nature, out of everything around us that is stunningly beautiful, God calls us his own. We are the apex of everything God created.

God's heart is found in creation. I don't mean just nature itself. I mean in the act of creation—to create something beautiful—in the act of restoration. The heart of God is found within mankind. We have the blueprint of God's work within us. We feel the most alive when we give away love freely to those who desperately need it. Isn't that exactly what God did for us? And that's why we find the love of God in giving ourselves away.

The next time we're sedated by our lack of guidance and staggering around wishing we knew God's plan for our lives, let's simply do what we know to do with what we have been given. Do what you can with what you have while you have it. In the midst of serving those around you, maybe you'll catch a glimpse of who you're designed to be and see God in the process. Don't overlook the simple things. Love is what will change the world. God's love is what will change the hearts of mankind.

You have a crucial role to play.

6 BRAVE THE UNKNOWN

In light of what we've learned so far, we should be propelled into action to overcome fear and the uncertainty we are bonded by when we choose to live based on Jesus' principles. To let fear hold us back is essentially telling God that he doesn't run this thing called life. When we let fear keep us in our safety zone, we are telling God that he isn't big enough to sustain us. God doesn't give you specific dreams and passions while asking something of you that he has not equipped you for. God asks of you what you've been given, to develop and implement in life-changing ways for others. When we refuse to step out and brave the unknown, we are telling God that he isn't good enough, that he doesn't care enough, and that we don't believe enough. We've been held back by fear long enough. We're missing out on the life that God has designed us for.

We can never brave the unknown if we are unwilling to be fundamentally changed. When you change your thinking, you will change your world. This change is not just in thought or knowing. This change is in your fundamental belief. You can know something and not change your actions, but to believe something means your actions and life will produce change because of that knowledge. Change does not occur without effort or the ability to do something differently, essentially to risk. If we continue to do what we have always done, we will continue to get the same results. It is only when we make a conscious change that we will experience change in our lives.

To follow the call of God is to live life in the unknown. We all long to be safe and live in abundance with all our needs supplied. The unknown goes against our basic survival instincts. We as humans have a need for security, which stretches throughout history and encompasses all cultures. But what happens when God calls us to leave that behind to follow his leading into the unacquainted world full of hesitations and unrelenting fears? Do we choose to listen or do we choose to stay in safety?

God has called us to journey into the unknown, relying on his strength, power, and provision alone in order to grow our faith and prove his faithfulness to us and those around us. To achieve ultimate growth we can no longer stand still and live in safety. The erroneous thing is that by playing safe, you will never accomplish much in life. You might live a good life and have great times, but you won't ever really live. You'll exist, but you won't live.

When God is calling us into the unknown, dangerous territory, he is calling us to be his light to the darkness. He is calling us to more, to what he specifically designed us for. He is calling us to love. Love isn't a complicated concept, though countless books have been written on the subject. Love is simply seeing a need and deciding to meet that need. To love others is to help others. Love is getting your hands dirty. It's not romantic as we dream it to be, but it's hard, painful, and selfless. You'll be placed in dangerous, uncomfortable, awkward and difficult spots if you choose to love others.

I've mistakenly always thought you had to know all the answers or have the problem figured out to help. Recently, I've discovered that's not the case, but that thinking was keeping me from helping the very people I desired to help. You don't need all the answers; you just need an attitude of non-stop compassion. People desire to be understood, to explain themselves, and to belong to community whether they're facing a difficult situation or not. When you come alongside someone, you are helping to ease their load even when you have no answers to their problem or situation. Many times people don't want the answers; they simply want to be known, understood and accepted.

I'm nervous to act in situations where I don't know what's going on. I think that's natural, but it's also paralyzing. We will never move unless we overcome or replace that fear with something else, or place that fear in something else. I'm the type of person who loves to have a plan to operate; I then develop that plan and a contingency plan and do what it takes in order for it to work. We have to stop waiting for that moment where all the points line up seamlessly and we feel this overwhelming sense to make our move. If we wait for that moment, it will never come. There comes an instant when you've done all you can do to prepare and you have to crash forward. Control what you can control and move forward. There will always be numerous variables outside of your power to control, but do what you can to optimize success on your end and then execute your move.

Many people feel the desire to help but aren't sure how to get involved. Don't be another person who talks about helping or says they wish they knew what to do. Our culture has enough of those people already. Go and be with that person. Spend time with them. Let them know you're thinking of them. Get your hands dirty; that's how change will take place, but only when we are able to overcome the initial fear that is holding us back. You're right. You don't know what's going to unfold or how that person will accept your offer, but you also won't ever know unless you choose to act. It doesn't take an expert; it just takes someone willing to try. You don't need a strategy; you just need the willingness to fail.

We all experience that moment of do or die. When you face that moment of decision, you have to be willing to take a risk or sit on the sidelines. It's impossible to do both. What I've come to find is that usually no one else is sure about it either. We all just pretend to be certain to boost our own self-assurance. No one knows the outcome. No one knows what the future holds. Those moments of decision happen to each one of us; they are just hidden under the surface, under the façade we create.

After you continually say no to opportunities, I believe those defining moments become fewer and far between. Maybe it's the prompting of the Holy Spirit, and maybe it's not. Regardless, when it's do or die, something is required of you whether you take a shot or not. The hard thing about responsibility is that you live with the decision you make. I'd much rather live with the decision to try to live all in as opposed to criticizing others from the sidelines.

One of the biggest uncertainties keeping me from taking opportunities is lack of confidence or inability. I didn't feel like I had what it took; I didn't feel like I was valuable or had anything worth contributing. After spending years on the sidelines, watching others make the big plays, I realized that because of who God is and who he told me I was that proved that I matter, that my story was worth telling. God spoke into my life telling me I had the ability, even when I didn't feel like it, to change someone's life. I had the power to alter history and influence culture because God gave me his Spirit and his love. Don't ever say you have nothing to offer to the world.

You'll never catch a wave if you don't venture into the ocean, and you'll never ride a mountain if you never strap your feet to the board. Everyone starts off in life as a beginner. Don't shy away because you've never done it before. Everyone at one point or another had never done it before either. We all had to start at the beginning. The professionals or experts are the ones who continue sacrificing and honing their skills to constantly progress. They suffer failure—they suffer defeat on major scales—but the difference is, they keep moving forward. You have to take a risk before you get the reward. You will fail. You will get bruised. And you will be changed in the process.

The unknown makes every adventure consequently much more exciting. My best friend Luke's famous quote is, "It's not an adventure until something goes wrong." When you come to the end of yourself, you have to rely on God alone and realize it's his power and influence that truly make the difference. When we come to the end of ourselves, we have to trust his plan and follow his lead into the wild. Many times in my life I have relied on my own strength and planning to get me through whatever situation was in front of me. Again and again, I find myself completely exhausted, not knowing if I'll be able to continue moving forward only to realize that I had forgotten the most critical part—relying on God's strength and not my own. The Bible paints vibrant stories of the times that God has brought his people back home to freedom and redemption—things that would be impossible for man and yet are easy for God. He doesn't sweat it when things fall through; he's got it. He's yet to be worried or perplexed by any problem; I forget that most days. I forget that God isn't worried about tomorrow; he isn't stressed out about what's happening in the news headlines; he is completely confident and able to sustain all things.

You only discover how to get over the fear of the unknown if you decide to stare down your fears instead of running away. The truth is you will never let go of fear entirely unless you take your fear off of the unknown and place that fear on God, the only one who charts the future, the one whose love overflows into our lives. We switch the objects of our fear. We never truly lose fear, or become fearless. We learn to place our insecurities and doubts into God and who he has called us to become. A change in thinking allows us the freedom to pursue what God has called us toward without regard to our circumstances. We can press onward because our faith isn't in ourselves anymore; it's in God's never-ending power. His arm is long enough to save, whether studying at university, serving people in South America, or traveling the globe. There has never been a place outside of God's grasp.

Maybe there have been many times before stepping outside of your comfort zone that you had a reality check and it seems God was pulling you toward the impossible. You think you cannot be good enough to accomplish this. You don't have what it takes to pull this off. You're not as good as others who God could use. Why would anyone listen to me? God could use someone else who has better talents, more experience, or is a better fit for the job. Over and over again, these questions run through my mind, especially during a meaningful project or a huge season of life. Doubt fills my mind. Anxiety overtakes me. I feel like I have nothing to offer; I feel like I'm too broken to make a difference, and I'm too jacked up for God to use me. It's one of Satan's greatest tactics at keeping us on the sidelines. The difference is that 5 percent make the leap of faith and 95 percent stand by critiquing.

If you believe what we've talked about so far, you're not only selling yourself short; you're selling God short. You are limiting his abilities to accomplish what he is asking you to pursue. It's selfish. We as humans have the inherent ability to circumnavigate any situation and make it about ourselves. We always bring it back to us and our own abilities while losing sight of God and his abilities.

In life you have to take a risk in order to get a return. You cannot continue to play safe and expect better results than what you have been getting in the past. It seems counterintuitive to put yourself in dangerous positions, but sometimes that's the only place we are going to grow as individuals or as a community. Bonds are forged and relationships are tested not when there are no problems and only smooth sailing, but when things get erratic and you have to place your full trust in someone else's abilities. A growing pattern happens when we are continually stretched to the end of ourselves and have to fully rely on God due to our inabilities and our weaknesses. This is why God's glory shines through us the most when we come to the end of ourselves and let God do his thing without our pride or selfish desires disrupting the process.

God desires to do so much more than you can imagine in your life, if you will only let him have all of you. In order to serve humbly like Jesus, we have to die to ourselves daily. There is no alternative. That is the only way to truly give everything, to serve, and love like Jesus did. He was on mission. Jesus knew his identity and was here to fulfill that purpose. Jesus didn't shy away from his mission because it was difficult, hard, or lonely. He had a bigger purpose and a reason to continue to serve and love others. He was a man on fire. Countless times in Scripture it talks of Jesus teaching as one who has authority, or the people were amazed at his power. These are phrases that express how passionate and enthusiastic Jesus was. He wasn't giving a decent effort, or doing better than the next guy. He was living all in. Jesus was vested in the pursuit of the broken and destitute.

It's not easy to sacrifice when we don't know the outcome of our actions. The high road is the one of discipline and sacrifice in order to love others. If we're honest, we're afraid of losing control. We like to know the plan and the relationship between our actions and the results they produce. In reality we don't have much control to begin with. We've fooled ourselves into thinking we have control over many aspects of life, but we essentially don't. Things can change in an instant. This life is fleeting.

You are not giving up your control and placing it in unknown hands; you are giving up your control and placing it in the best hands possible—the very hands of the living God. There has never been a better person to place your future in than the very being who created it all. It's difficult to let go of our grasp, and it's something I struggle to do every day, but when I have the perspective and belief that God is who he says he is, then naturally out of that relationship I trade in my worry and stress for freedom and peace of mind.

When we are afraid to take risks, our relationship with Jesus suffers. It's impossible to grow if we are unwilling to be vulnerable about who we are. Until we come to a point where we can be open, our relationship will remain stagnant. Fear will hold us back from becoming who God has designed us to be. We don't have to be fearful of who we are or who we're not; God desires us as we are. Jesus is interceding for us at the right hand of God. We are not perfect, but daily we are being renewed and transformed into a better image of God. We are image bearers of God himself.

My lack of trust in God's provisions is what feeds my insecurities and longing for safety, holding me back from taking action. If I fully placed my trust in Jesus, I should never have to worry about the future or the wild unknown. Instead, most days I'm stressed out and continuously planning in order to avoid failure or a costly mistake. God tells us we don't need to worry our lives away but that he takes care of the birds of the air and how much more will he take care of his own children.

My initial reaction is to work harder, work longer, and figure it out myself—whereas God already has the answer and the plan. I'm too stubborn to stop and realize that God has life on track, and I'm too prideful to ask for help. It's the problem of pride; I want to do it on my own without the help from others or from God. I want to figure it out. I want the praise. I want to be my own hero. In these moments I lose sight of the mission and my fears surround me, pushing me back to my loving Father.

I call it the parachute moment. It's that moment after you've jumped from the plane and you have roughly 58 seconds to realize that if this parachute doesn't open, it's all over. You enjoy those 58 seconds immensely. Putting yourself in that situation of trust—the moment of do or die—is difficult because it all comes down to the parachute opening. There's not much more to do if that doesn't happen. The same goes for rock climbing. All of your faith is placed in your belayer, the person below you making sure you don't fall to an untimely death. A lot of people will make it to the top of a route and hesitate before coming down. The hesitation comes because at that moment in time, their life is in someone else's hands, and that's terrifying. It's that moment where you think, *Is this going to work out or not?* God desires us to live in that state—this constant state of placing our lives in his hands. If God wasn't a part of what you're doing, would it fail? That's one of the questions that has defined my life.

Before enormous moments in life I think we hit a section of time I call the moment of truth. It's that feeling of sickness, of inabilities and insecurities that arise before a particular event in life, that has consequences that will change the outcome of your life.

In the world of action sports, athletes are faced with this moment of truth day in and day out. That is if you're willing to push yourself beyond what you've previously done. You've been talking about this moment all morning while riding the mountain. You've wanted to hit this specific feature, jump or rail, all day. Now it's time to step up, strap in and do it. You're sitting at the top of the take-off, strapping into your bindings, debating in your head if it's worth the risk. Should you go for it and possibly land it or simply go for something that you've done before?

You're rapidly approaching the jump when you have that feeling in your stomach and the weight in your gut. Your knees are shaking and your heart feels like it's going to beat out of your chest cavity. You have a decision to make: commit and keep going or bail and stay in the safe zone and ride around the feature. You only have a few seconds to decide. You know if you ride around the jump, you will be flooded with disappointment, but you will also be safe. It's a hard choice to make. Life is made up of a balance between these two decisions.

Along your journey there will come plenty of moments where you are faced with decisions that don't have clear-cut answers, and it's always terrifying. You have the choice to pursue something you were made for or the choice of taking the easy way out. Regardless, you have to make a choice either way. You face the hardest choices when you don't know the outcome. I don't know if I'm going to land this jump or break a bone, and that's a choice I have to make. I'm not advising you to do anything you haven't prepared to do. You can't just go for it. You have to train and prepare for whatever task you're facing, but there is a time that you will have the necessary training and the foundation laid to go for it. If you can't ride well, don't hit the terrain park. If you can make it down double blacks with ease, I'd say it's about time to ride over and hit some jumps and touch some rails.

It's still a terrifying event. Every time I approach a rail, my mind starts playing games, imagining that I'll clip my board and land face first on the cold hard steel. But again there is a moment where I could ride around the launching pad and just avoid the feature altogether, or I could face my fears and progress in my riding abilities. I won't tell you it's easy, or that I'm good at it. I'm not. But I spent time learning all the fundamentals; I train hard off the snow; I'm physically and mentally fit, and most importantly, I'm willing to take a risk.

I don't understand why I'm built this way, but almost always when doing anything exciting I am coaxed into pushing myself beyond what I've previously accomplished whether that means trying new features, riding new routes, or anything that I haven't done yet. I can't leave until I do it. Frequently, it doesn't end well. The pain and bruises are worth the effort, knowing I pushed myself in a new direction. I walk away knowing that I faced my fear and I risked progressing to the next level. When you make it to the other side, often times you look back, discovering that it wasn't that big of a mountain to begin with.

Almost anything beneficial in life comes down to a do-it-or-not decision. Your adrenaline is flowing freely and you can barely see straight. Your knees are shaking; your stomach is cramping, and it's in these moments that we decide who we are going to become. You have to commit. You'll hear this so many times that you just laugh. You've just got to commit. Just commit, man. Lying in pain after face-planting on the cold, hard ice, I hear, "You didn't commit, man." "You gotta commit, bro." It's the man who is willing to die for what he believes who will make all the difference. Look at the life of Paul; take a look at what he says here in 2 Corinthians 11:23-27:

I have worked much harder, been in prison more frequently, been flogged more severely, and been exposed to death again and again. Five times I received from the Jews the forty lashes minus one. Three times I was beaten with rods, once I was pelted with stones, three times I was shipwrecked, I spent a night and a day in the open sea, I have been constantly on the move. I have been in danger from rivers, in danger from bandits, in danger from my fellow Jews, in danger from Gentiles; in danger in the city, in danger in the country, in danger at sea; and in danger from false believers. I have labored and toiled and have often gone without sleep; I have known hunger and thirst and have often gone without food; I have been cold and naked.

Paul was a man by anyone's standards. To think about this list and for him to continue pushing forward is irrational. But how was he able to do that and continue pushing boundaries? It's all because of his mindset. He counted all things a loss for the sake of knowing Christ Jesus. All was less than rubbish compared to knowing and serving Jesus. Do you think he would have willingly risked his life again and again if he didn't have something better to live for? I don't think so. It all comes down to our motivation and our mindset. When you know the outcome is worth the investment, the discipline and the sacrifice take care of themselves.

What you fear is what you will worship. We can clearly see that Paul didn't fear the government; he didn't fear the elements, nor did he fear the unknown. It's not that he wasn't afraid; Paul wasn't super-human. He just believed in a God who is superior to his circumstances. I'm sure there were plenty of times Paul was terrified. When you look at that list, any rational being would have been. That fear didn't stop Paul though because Paul was able to count all else a loss for the surpassing greatness of knowing Jesus Christ. I don't think he even considered this a sacrifice. God was able to use Paul to change the world, partly because Paul was able to face his fears and place his trust in the God who provides and protects. It doesn't mean Paul never felt the infliction of pain, the isolation of loneliness, the sting of betrayal—because Paul did feel that. But Paul didn't let the circumstances that he was placed in define him; he let God do that.

Remember the story of Jesus calming the storm? The one where the disciples were flipping out, thinking they were going to die, and Jesus was taking a nap. That reminds me of my own life. I tend to freak out and let my fears get the best of me, thinking, *This is it; this is how it ends.* And Jesus is just over there sleeping like it's no big deal. How many times have I cried out to God, "Don't you care? Don't you see what's happening?" When the storms in my life are raging, when I think I'm nearing all I can handle, I forget this passage; I forget the power of God. I focus on my own problems and take my eyes off of Jesus and his power. It says the disciples were amazed and asked, "What kind of man is this? Even the winds and the waves obey him?" (Matthew 8:27).

With a meaningful life, risk will always be required. And the thing with risk is, sometimes it works out and sometimes it doesn't. If you're waiting for a 100 percent risk-free opportunity, it won't ever come. There's risk involved with everything—from the small things to the big things. And there is no bigger risk than love. The thing about love is that in the end, you might get hurt. There's only one way to avoid that, and that is to never put yourself out there, to never love. When we let fear hold us back, we're missing opportunities to grow close with Jesus.

We were made to be brave. We were designed to rely on God's perfection. We weren't made to play it safe, holed up in our suburbs watching life being lived by characters on TV. God created us to do good works and to shine glory back to him. You were made for something greater.

Yeah, you're right it's not safe. Life wasn't intended to be safe. When things are safe, when things are average, when things go as planned—you don't grow as a person; you don't get excited. You just continue moving on in life without enthusiasm. You keep wasting the life that you have on trivial pursuits. The dreams and passions that God has given to us will take all we are in order to fulfill, but we have to be willing to risk everything to know what could be.

People will take risks for what they believe in. This is where faith comes into play—weighing the cost of the decision to play it safe or try to swim. A lot of times you won't have clear answers. You won't hear a thundering voice, and you'll simply have a sense about it, a small inclination to choose the path on the right over the path on the left. It's something inside of you that points you in a certain direction even though you know it's unsafe, it's dangerous, but it's what you were created to do. You won't know the outcome. People will disagree with your choice. People won't understand. God calls us to places beyond ourselves, beyond our earthly logic, and beyond the mundane.

One of my favorite responses by Jesus was, "Come and see." He didn't give a detailed plan with a step-by-step itinerary, but simply invited people to join what he was doing. What would happen if we never decided to start this journey? Where would we be if we were too startled to begin? Jesus gives us the invitation. John Stott said, "His authority on earth allows us to dare to go to all the nations. His authority in heaven gives us our only hope of success. And his presence with us leaves us with no other choice."

This is the intimidating part, the dangerous part of the journey into the unknown. We don't know where God is calling us or what God is preparing for us to accomplish. What if God is going to ask me to spend the rest of my life living like the homeless, forsaking the comforts of security of a nine-to-five job in order to reach his children living on the streets? There are so many "what if" questions in life. It all comes down to these questions: Am I willing to surrender and let Jesus have all of me in order that God may be glorified in my life? It's easy to read and to watch other people do it, but me? I have dreams, I have goals, I want an easy life. I want a beautiful wife with an abundance of children, and I want a nice house in a safe city near the beach. God, are you asking me to sacrifice those things and risk my dreams to bring you glory? What if God is calling us to more than we ever imagined?

You have to decide what kind of story you want to live. I can't imagine anything worse than a life of regret. Don't believe the lie for a second when you think you're missing out because you're trusting God over what society is telling you. God created adventure; you're not going to want to miss this.

7 PEOPLE ARE PEOPLE

When I pause from the crazy busy moments of life and breathe, I find that life isn't actually all about me. Those other people have stories, ambitions, and dreams also. They're not just cashiers, car salesmen, bank tellers, or nurses; they are people just like me with flaws, fears, imperfections, and dreams they're chasing down. Everyone has a story. I've discovered that most people have exhilarating stories when I take the necessary time to listen. I have been astonished time after time, even after knowing someone for years, when I hear a story they have never shared with me before. I wondered why they had never shared that part of their life or the experiences they lived through. It's in those moments that I realized maybe I wasn't actually listening to what they were communicating in words or in their silence. I was listening to simply respond.

If we are unwilling to take the time to listen and penetrate beyond the superficial surface of life, we will miss out on the best of what people have to offer. People are more than the clothes they wear, the cars they drive, the houses they reside in, or the job titles they possess. People are composed of abundantly more than we give them credit for. A deeper conversation is weaving our stories together. It's time we step out and listen more intently.

It's no secret that we have a tendency to label people. Some might call it judging, but in reality we label people into categories based on our own life experiences and expect them to be the same as the last person we filed into that strictly defined category. I don't think it's wrong to label people into certain categories, we are just sorting people like we sort everything else in life. The error is that we're missing out on growing from people's stories and not connecting in deeper ways when we don't take the necessary time to know someone. It's incredible the amount we can learn when we stop the glorification of busy and genuinely listen to those around us. Everyone has something to offer and to teach if we connect past the surface subjects that predominately hijack our conversations.

Everyone comes from extraordinary circumstances if we dig deep enough. We all have different life experiences and passions that we can all share with each other and grow from because of our differences. That's the power of diversity. We've lost the value of diversity due to our culture relegating the meaning of the word to just skin color and nothing more. When different cultures fuse, we can all learn and grow from one another's life experiences; we will find value in diversity. Even though we are only 18 months apart, my older brother and I are completely different despite having close to the exact same upbringing, the same friend groups, and playing the same sports. We were created to be different.

I wanted to share a few stories from my own experiences in life where I decided to listen to other peoples' stories before making a judgment, and the immense impact it has had on me because of that simple decision to listen. These are real people with real stories that bleed of a common humanity. When we strip away the walls, we find our stories aren't entirely that different.

Debilitated by severe depression since the age of nine, you might never see him with two free hands since one hand is always clutching a wrinkled brown bag covering the medicine inside. The story traces back to a certain event in his young life, which he can never rid his mind of. He can't stop the memories or the feelings of what happened that day in his own living room. If we had met out on the street or in a bar, I would have labeled him as an everyday alcoholic who was heavy on the bottle.

I didn't meet him in the street though; I met him in the psych ward. He had been diagnosed with depressive disorder with suicidal ideation.

The only time he didn't feel the immense pain from life was when he was holding a bottle. He never had a recollection of a good memory in his entire life. He was over 40 years old when we spoke during his initial psych evaluation. Can you imagine having no recollection of anything positive in over 40 years of life? What could possibly be so atrocious in this man's story to cause something of this magnitude? At first glance I thought he was just another alcoholic.

He began to tell his story. What he had to say would forever change my life. He said, "I watched as my father held a gun to my mother's face and pulled the trigger. After shooting my mother, my father looked directly into my eyes and told me, 'This is your fault.' My father then put the gun to his own head and killed himself. I was nine years old that day both my parents died. I was standing in the living room surrounded by my parent's bloody bodies—alone."

She was a beautiful girl—one of the most beautiful girls I have ever known. She was continually in and out of relationships with all kinds of guys, moving on from one to the next in a matter of days. She was an all-American beauty, but she found her worth in unhealthy relationships with abusive boyfriends, amidst other things.

She took me to the house where it all happened. The house sat proudly on the left side of the street in this quiet, small-town American city. It wasn't a house any different than the other hundreds of houses in that neighborhood. She pulled the SUV over and opened up to me about her past, telling me this was the exact place where she had been raped as a child over and over again. I wasn't ready for that on that sunny Saturday afternoon. Suddenly, everything inside of me stopped. I had chills running down my spine, and the sky seemed to blacken with every word falling out of her mouth.

A female babysitter had sexually abused her for years as a child. She didn't know what was happening in the beginning; her babysitter just called it playtime. It went on for years before she moved out of town and away with her family. Her family never knew until she was 19 when she had the courage and support she needed in order to tell her family and to seek the appropriate treatment for all the trauma that happened to her.

She had a colorful history of sleeping around with different guys because that was when she didn't feel the pain and the horror of her past. Maybe she was labeled a whore and called worse names than that behind her back. Maybe we wouldn't agree with her lifestyle choices. We might even look down at her situation if she were to be the one to stumble through the doors any given Sunday, but there is always more going on than what we can perceive on the surface level of things.

She's different now. Jesus found her and is actively rescuing and redeeming who she is. She's no longer stuck in the pain and horror but is finding her identity in who God has designed her to be. God is working through her and her past in order to use it to save other girls who have gone through or are currently going through the same devastating circumstances. She's a major activist in the fight against human trafficking. She is able to help girls escape the terrible tragedy they have to live through on a daily basis. Jesus is redeeming and using the pain of her past to improve and fight for a better future for others.

It was a little past one in the morning when I got that slip of pink paper that would drastically change my life. The pink paper was the new admit paperwork for a patient coming to my medical-surgical floor through the emergency department. All the pink slip of paper said was his name, age, weight, and his diagnosis, which was homicidal/suicidal. That's all we knew about this kid.

It was my assignment to sit with him through the night in the hospital room in order to make sure we both made it to 0730 the next morning, alive. I cleared the room of anything he could use to harm himself or others. By the time I had the room prepared, the transport team was arriving from the emergency department.

Many people write these off with a label and a deep sigh, a mumbling of words like, "Just another suicidal patient," followed by a shrug of the shoulders. If you took the time to listen to his story and the experiences he'd had to live through, you would have seen things differently. Luckily, I was placed in that spot for a reason. It was no coincidence that I was scheduled for that shift that night.

He had never known a time in his life where his mother's boyfriend wasn't beating him every night. He'd never known his mom without two black eyes. He might not even recognize her if she ever got away and didn't have a swollen face with bruises from all the beatings. If it wasn't enough to watch your own mother be furiously beaten to a state of unconsciousness night after night, and stepping in whenever he could to take the beatings for her, he was being bullied and harassed at school. He reached out to the teachers, to the staff, and to other students, but no one listened; no one cared enough to step in. The bullying didn't end. The beatings didn't stop. He couldn't even escape the unbearable pain at school. I'm not sure which one hurt worse: the emotional pain from the bullying every day at school or the physical pain from the beatings and cigarette marks every night at home.

He continued to reach out to anybody at the school who would listen to stop the bullying—not even accounting for the beatings—but simply the bullying at school from other kids. That's all he wanted. He could endure the beatings night after night, but the bullying from the kids at school, that's another story. I've found that wounds on the inside are commonly more hurtful than the scars on the outside.

No one listened, no one cared, and nothing changed. Nothing happened until one day he couldn't take it anymore. He did exactly what all people do when they cry out and no one listens—they resort to violence. He stood up in front of his classroom and started flipping desks and throwing anything he could manage to get his hands on. He yelled at the teachers and the other students to whom he cried out to day after day. He ran outside and declared that he would kill those who didn't listen to his pleas for help, and then he would end his own life.

HE WASN'T EVEN 12 YEARS OLD YET.

I wish I could tell you that everything worked out and this kid became the exception to the abusive situation, went on to graduate high school, received a full-ride scholarship to university and ended up changing that situation for so many others dealing with abuse on a daily basis. But honestly, I don't know what happened after the few hours I spent with him on that day when it all climaxed. I'd like to believe that what I did and said had a lasting impact and I was able to reflect God's love for him even through that difficult time, but I don't know the outcome of his story. I don't know what happened to him after those early morning hours we spent together.

If it's like anything I imagine, he most likely spent some time in a pediatric psych ward and was placed right back into the midst of that family and school situation—only this time it would be worse, much worse. Now he was labeled, diagnosed. He would cry out and still no one would listen. Maybe he got out though, maybe a foster family took him in. But those stats aren't overwhelmingly positive either, especially if you're labeled as homicidal and suicidal.

Another thing I wish I could say is that this is an isolated incident. But it's not. We see it all the time. Our emergency departments are overflowing with suicidal ideation, drug overdoses, and explosive disorders from children aged 13 and under. This is happening before kids even reach high school. I don't think Cincinnati, Ohio, is the exception either. This is an epidemic and it's happening around the nation.

Everyone has a story. Maybe it's simply time we started listening. Don't be too quick to write others off. We all need help and community on this journey we share together. You'd be surprised how fast you can find something in common with any person you meet. Start viewing strangers as friends and your attitude, and your life will change for the better. We still have so much left to learn.

Never fool yourself into thinking that people are entirely that different from each other. We all need the same basic things in life. We all desire many of the same goals out of life, such as family, friends, love, healthy relationships and more, just like most humans on the planet. We only really differ on a few things such as worldview, personal desires, and life experiences. These can be huge differences, so don't misunderstand me, but there are common threads of humanity running through all our lives.

Without the backstory of one another's lives, it's easy to write people out of the books. We see them make terrible mistakes and unwise choices and instantly project our own life experiences and upbringing onto that person. How could they have done that? But isn't it true that we've all made immoral decisions and appalling life choices? You can write those less fortunate off by saying they made unwise choices and lacked the necessary discipline, but through the process you will be changed and moved toward a more cynical view of others. You will stop loving others and start criticizing instead.

Perhaps they themselves regret the situations they are living in. Maybe they didn't expect to be the one to have to decide between a baby and a career. Maybe they had to decide between tuition and food for their family, and maybe they did make a bad decision, the wrong choice. Don't think for a second Jesus ever wrote them off. And if Jesus didn't write them off, we shouldn't either.

At dawn he appeared again in the temple courts, where all the people gathered around him, and he sat down to teach them. The teachers of the law and the Pharisees brought in a woman caught in adultery. They made her stand before the group and said to Jesus, "Teacher, this woman was caught in the act of adultery. In the Law Moses commanded us to stone such women. Now what do you say?" They were using this question as a trap, in order to have a basis for accusing him.

But Jesus bent down and started to write on the ground with his finger. When they kept on questioning him, he straightened up and said to them, "Let any one of you who is without sin be the first to throw a stone at her." Again he stooped down and wrote on the ground. At this, those who heard began to go away one at a time, the older ones first, until only Jesus was left, with the woman still standing there. Jesus straightened up and asked her, "Woman, where are they? Has no one condemned you?"

"No one, sir," she said. "Then neither do I condemn you," Jesus declared. "Go now and leave your life of sin."[1]

---

[1] John 8:2-11

Maybe we're collectively in the same boat trying desperately to get to the same place of wholeness and hope. We have different ways to numb the pain, survive our daily struggles, and feel alive, but at the end of the day people are people. We're born, we breathe, we eat, we drink, we live, and we die. We all desire to make a difference in whatever way we can. We are all in need of a savior—someone or something outside of us that can redeem our situation—whether we are the ones who realize it or not.

People are people. One of the most impactful lessons I've learned—whether that was spending time in Mexico, Nicaragua, or Tanzania—was that no matter what culture or people group you are surveying, assessing, or interacting with, we all long for the same basic things. We all desire to be loved, to be successful, to be surrounded with family and friends, to see the ones we love thrive, to provide for those around us, and we all want peace. These are all common desires we share as human beings. People want to belong. People want to be loved. People desire to be useful and have an impact on their surroundings. We long to know that we matter and that we have purpose.

Understanding leads us to a place of love. When we understand others, we quickly turn from a stance of criticism to one of compassion. Jesus understood people. He cared. He cared about the big things and the small things alike. Jesus cared for the everyday people, for all people. He spent time with the broken. He didn't just write a new formula and take our issues away. He didn't hand out pills to fix people's problems. He spent quality time with people, listening to their stories, understanding on a deep level, and peering beyond their current situation to matters of the heart. He didn't see people as problems or subjects to rule over or govern. Jesus isn't that kind of a king.

Instead he viewed people as his own family, his own brothers and sisters. He loved fiercely, and he proved that love.

Life transforms drastically when we start viewing people as God does and not just as a means to our own selfish ends. It's a magical unfolding that takes place when we see people in the correct light, not competition on the totem pole but as vital community. You start caring again. You start feeling again. You come out of the paralytic state to feel alive when you love others. Your heart is changed in the process. Opportunities are endless when you start viewing people through the lens of redemption. There are no longer dirty, broken people—they are loved and desired by God himself. Shouldn't that be enough for us also?

These principles are the foundation of a powerful encounter with my new friend Rhamos. It was a very unlikely encounter on all levels. I was staying out in California for a few days with my Californian family, taking life easy, surfing, and having some crazy adventures. They decided to go camping at Big Bear over the weekend, and I decided to stay back in order to work on some writing and job applications and to make sure everything was in place for my college graduation, but instead I took off for the beach to go surfing. I threw everything in the back of the SUV and headed to Malibu. I was pulling into the Malibu State Beach parking area in order to park, unload the surfboards, and surf the iconic beach break Surfrider.

As I approached the gate, I saw the attendant and started getting my wallet out to pay the ten bucks to park for the day. The usual small talk about the weather, how his day is going, and so forth naturally ensued as with most fleeting encounters in my life. He then asked me how my day was progressing, and here I am pulling in to surf in Malibu—one of the most consistent waves in the world—so naturally I'm stoked for what's about to happen the rest of the morning and afternoon. This is the exact spot where surfing exploded here in the States, so I'm pretty high on life to surf such a historic and fun wave. This is the actualization of a dream. Usually, I respond by saying something along the lines of great, phenomenal, fantastic or can't complain to almost anyone who asks that question. From the slough of choices that day, and I was feeling all those things, for whatever reason I picked, "Can't complain." And that's when he stopped. He hung onto the phrase "Can't complain." Time froze. He started interrogating me and kept probing deeper about that phrase and how I used it.

I suppose I should back up and inform you that he was just the parking lot attendant, working—doing his thing—handing out parking passes and exchanging money. But I have this mindset of treating everyone, and I mean everyone, I come into contact with each day with the upmost respect in every single encounter, whether that's my mom or the guy making French fries at McDonald's. When you start seeing people as people, it's essentially not that difficult. Because that guy making the fries doesn't actually want to be making fries at 2 a.m. in the morning for some grouchy customer, believe it or not. I'm sure he actually wants to be asleep but can't afford to sleep, so he's working midnights at McDonald's. And that's not a great place to be in life, and I'm sure that's not quite his dream job either. Now you have the opportunity to peer into his life, not as the dude making fries, but as another human living his own story. Maybe he's going through a really rough time and needs this as a second gig and chose McDonald's over selling drugs, or he's paying his own way through university. You'll never really know unless you ask or take the time to listen. And you'll never ask if you never care. And you won't ever care unless you understand and see him as a whole person, another human who has a story that might be remarkably similar to your own.

That's a long way of saying people are people and we do this thing called life together. We ought to start treating people like family—with love and support—instead of considering them enemies, marked with bitterness. Take time and connect with people. It'll change your life and maybe even theirs in the process.

Back to the storyline. So here I am paying for parking and talking with Rhamos about the weather, his day, and his job. The conversation gets heavy. I love deep conversations; it's the best thing in the world to me. It's how I'm wired to connect with others. He started asking me where I learned at such a young age not to complain about life's situations. And I was taken aback, thinking, *I don't know if I ever learned that really. I'm definitely still trying to figure it out.* I just got sick and tired of people complaining all the time and made up my mind to be different, changing my attitude not to complain. He was astounded that I learned that lesson at the age of 22.

Clearly, this conversation marked a huge point in his own story since he was asking intently about an attitude and decision not to complain. I then simply flipped the question and asked him the same thing. He told me it took him 55 years, a stroke, and 3 days stuck in a hospital bed to learn the lesson of not complaining.

He used to have high blood pressure, which is what led to the stroke. Now that he stopped complaining and changed his attitude, he hasn't had high blood pressure since. And this is all minor compared to the rest of the conversation that followed.

He went on talking and I could clearly tell he wasn't from the States so I prodded and asked where he was born and raised. He proceeded to inform me that he was born and raised in Ethiopia. He was an Ethiopian refugee sent to the States by the government in 1983. And he's absolutely loved it ever since.

"The land of opportunity," he said. I asked what he did for work and he answered that he was a general contractor for 22 years in the greater L.A. area. After those 22 years he said things unfortunately didn't work out. I asked if he was able to visit his homeland of Ethiopia very often. He emphatically told me he just returned a few weeks ago. I was intrigued. He was eager to share and the words he said blew me away. He said, "I have been going back every few months for years now and I have planted over 1,000,000 trees in my home country." One million trees, I couldn't believe it. He's the founder of an NGO, which works in conjunction with the United Nations, developing fruit orchards in order to help produce a natural source of nutritious food for Ethiopia's vulnerable people groups. Not only that, but he also said, "I'm not planting trees; I'm planting unity." Through his organization he brings Christians and Muslims together—two warring tribes unified together to plant trees and bring peace to the region—while providing viable nutrient-dense food for generations to come.

And the sad thing is that I almost missed this human connection like I'm sure thousands of people have before who have driven through that parking lot. I almost missed it to go surfing. I never would have known this man's remarkable story in life if I didn't stop and listen. I almost labeled him like everyone else, just some old immigrant at the parking ticket booth who doesn't have a job that pays well or higher education or whatever. And I would have been so wrong. He's a man who is making a sustainable impact on millions of lives. He's changing the outcome of generations to come.

Everyone has a story; let's start listening.

8 AUTHENTIC COMMUNITY

Life wasn't intended to be lived alone. We clearly see this principle from the very beginning when God decided to make Adam a companion. Life is meant to be lived in community, to be shared, to be collectively appreciated by all. Even Jesus had community. If the Son of God was intent on community, how much more so should we be? If Jesus was about it, we should be about it. Jesus had his crew and I can only imagine what it would have been like to experience everyday life with the most influential man in history. How crazy would that experience have been?

One of my favorite verses in the Bible is the last verse of the Book of John. It states, "Jesus did many other things as well. If every one of them were written down, I suppose that even the whole world would not have room for the books that would be written." Can you imagine the stories we've never heard and the miracles that aren't retold in the Bible? We have a minuscule glimpse into the life of Christ and the community he shared with his disciples, but there is so much more to the story that we have not heard yet. To walk and talk with the very Son of God would have been such an unbelievable experience. It's hard to fathom the stories the disciples got to live on a daily basis while walking with Jesus.

Again and again, Jesus brings the disciples back to the heart of the matter. This kind of community helps to ground us and keep us focused on what matters in life, on what our stories are all about. When disputes broke out among the disciples about who is the greatest, he grounded them back to the truth. The disciples commonly lost focus, just like we do, but community brings us back to the source of what matters. True community challenges you, keeps you honest, humbles you, encourages you in your walk with God, and helps you walk the narrow path. That's community. It's hard, it's honest, it's difficult, and it's family. How vital community is for our growth is easily overlooked. Community is what we were created for.

People don't thrive while living life on their own. Scientific studies substantiate that our health and happiness are directly correlated to our social relationships. Social relationships can be the sole predictor of a healthy life as current research continues to reveal:

Social relationships—both quantity and quality—affect mental health, health behavior, physical health, and mortality risk. Sociologists have played a central role in establishing the link between social relationships and health outcomes, identifying explanations for this link, and discovering social variation (e.g., by gender and race) at the population level. Studies show that social relationships have short- and long-term effects on health, for better and for worse, and that these effects emerge in childhood and cascade throughout life to foster cumulative advantage or disadvantage in health.[1]

[1] http://www.ncbi.nlm.nih.gov/pmc/articles/PMC3150158) (Umberson D, Montez JK. Social Relationships and Health: A Flashpoint for Health Policy. Journal of health and social behavior. 2010;51(Suppl):S54-S66. doi:10.1177/0022146510383501.

Research is beginning to reveal what we have known from the beginning, that we, as humans, were created for and thrive in a context of community. Think about the times in life that actually mattered; I bet it was a life experience that was shared intimately with others. Perhaps it was sitting around the campfire with friends, holidays with family, or serving alongside others you love for a common goal. It's in these moments of time that I am able to feel that this is what life is about. This earthly community is a small reflection of the glory of God's community and what we were ultimately created for—relationships.

It's quite rare in our country to take a gap year between high school and university, but it's more common in many countries around the globe. You either travel, backpack, work or visit with family or friends internationally for a year or two in order to experience life outside of what you know before starting your career or going back to higher education. In America, we highly value a structured system where high school students are funneled directly into university. They are given only a few months between graduation and beginning studies at university. Those few months are commonly known as "the last few months of freedom." Fortunately for me, my family encouraged me to take a gap year. So I packed my bags and headed to the untamed wilderness of Montana.

I knew I wanted to take a year off to focus on who I was and what I desired out of life. My mom and dad both encouraged me to apply to the Montana Wilderness School of the Bible (MWSB). I was accepted with a few weeks to spare and decided to bite the bullet and headed off for a year in Montana. I'd never been that far west before. I didn't know anything or anyone in Montana, but I was ready for a change in scenery and some wild adventures.

I had no idea how transformative that year would be. It completely shook everything I'd ever known. It was the wildest, hardest, and most beneficial time of my life. I almost died twice, but those are minor details. This place was about experiencing the beauty and wildness of the God who created the vast wilderness of the world, all we see and feel. I can't adequately summarize all that transpired at MWSB, but I know it crosses my thoughts daily even after six years since graduation. It was truly the best time of my life. That year in the wilderness built the solid foundation for everything that has followed since.

MWSB was the closest to a heavenly community that I believe I'll ever experience on earth. The campus was made up of six dorms, a recreation building, dining hall, three staff houses, and the chapel building where classes were held Monday through Friday. Our class was composed of sixty students from all over the world. We started as strangers and ended as family. If you ever felt that connection that comes at summer camp or a mission trip, it was like that except for an entire year. It's impossible to paint the picture for you with words. It is truly something you have to experience. The fact that we lived life together, almost died together, had the most intimate conversations, and withdrew from modern-day worries and technology to pursue a foundation of Jesus—it's something that I will never forget or experience on this side of heaven again. Those were my people. It was intentional community searching intimately for Jesus.

The drive back home to Ohio was the hardest drive of my life. It was hard to leave my family behind as we dispersed back across the globe. We graduated on a beautiful April Saturday morning, snow still saturating the ground with 2-3 inches from the evening before. After the closing ceremony and receiving my diploma came the tears, the hugs, the kisses and the heartbreak of leaving this community behind. I threw my snowboard, my rifle, my backpacking gear and everything else I had accumulated over the year in the wilderness into the back of our Kia Soul, and my mom and I set off for home. I'd been on numerous trips before around the world visiting Africa or Europe, but I knew this time coming home would be different. I was changed. I was different.

Driving back through the plains of North Dakota, the tears wouldn't stop falling from my eyes. My hands wouldn't stop shaking, and it felt like everything had been ripped away. It was hard coming back to a distracted, self-seeking, empty society to pursue higher education at a large public university. One day I was the closest to heaven I'll ever be on this earth, and the next moment it felt like it was all behind me. I was alone on an enormous campus of 43,000 students. I had the closest family of 59 other guys and girls, striving after the Lord on a passionate journey in the wilderness of Montana. Next I found myself looking around the university campus asking, where did it all go?

University was difficult. It wasn't difficult because of my studies; it was difficult because I was constantly surrounded by thousands of people but at the same time felt isolated and alone. I was alone on this journey to find myself, my purpose, my calling in life, and to figure out the next steps. This was a massive transition period of life when you decide what your life is going to be about. It's a very exhilarating part of life, but at the same time difficult because you're solely responsible for yourself and your actions. It's a huge opportunity to grow and develop into the person you desire to become.

Life is challenging. Life is more challenging alone. Life shared in the context of community is life as it was designed to be. Life lived alone is a life wasted. I walked this path filled with darkness, loneliness and pain for three out of four years at university. Although the pain was at times unbearable on my own strength, I wouldn't trade this period of my life for a different story. These trials that I walked through grew me into the man God has called me to be. He brought me through as a stronger and better man for walking through the pain. He brought me to the other side of my struggle a different man. God showed me the importance of community and the impact it has on life's trajectory.

Everyone needs a wolf pack to belong to—a crew of people to have your back, put an arm around you and tell you, "I got you." One of the greatest things about working in a hospital setting is that people finally get serious about issues in life. It's not just a game anymore. Perspectives change rapidly when people are dying. And when people are dying, I listen. They have nothing left to lose; therefore, they hold nothing back. Most dying patients have said the one thing they would go back and change was to live life with a team. They wish they were closer with their family, their children, and with their friends. They all said they wished they would have been closer to the people who mattered and spent less time working for material possessions and what society commonly persuades us are important achievements and instead invested their time on intimate relationships.

For the past four years I've struggled to find community that engages me on a deep level. I'm not looking for a social club; I'm searching for people who are desperate for Jesus. Everywhere I searched I couldn't find anything that held my attention or my drive enough to convince me to commit. Small group after small group, church after church, ministry after ministry, nothing seemed relevant to me. For whatever reason, it all seemed dead to me; there was no substance. Other people enjoyed it, and I'm glad they did, but I didn't find anything worthwhile in my search for something more. I knew there was more since I had experienced actual community. It was attainable and not just this romantic idea of community. I had the real thing in Montana. This could be done—not some shallow misrepresentation of community, not a replication—the real thing was attainable.

It seemed like I was simply wasting hours of my life every week at a small group where we'd mainly talk about women, pornography, lust, homework and sometimes Jesus for a few minutes. It wasn't really my scene. I was looking for answers—for truth—not some dudes who claimed one thing and lived something else entirely. I just knew there was more to community than this.

Our generation struggles to find a real community to belong to, to help us along in the journey, to bring people together. We struggle. I know we struggle because it's been a re-occurring theme in my life. I've been in and out of churches, ministries, and small groups, drifting around trying to find my place. It's not that I wasn't accepted, except for the times I definitely wasn't accepted. And I realize you may not know me personally, but I'm generally accepted wherever my feet land me. It was that I couldn't find others to connect with in a meaningful way. I didn't have a lot of time to waste sitting around once a week sipping coffee having superficial conversations about Jesus without any significance. They may have talked about Jesus, but it never seemed like anyone actually walked with Jesus. There's a major difference between those two things.

I was tired of wasting my time and scheduling my day around small groups only to realize I wasn't getting anything out of it besides frustration. I don't mean to criticize small groups or ministries because I realize and understand the importance and how vital these communities are. I know how vital community is because I've been through that experience where I didn't have the community I desperately needed.

God uses our pain to bring about redemption. God always has a way to turn our wounds into meaningful aspects of our life's story. Now I know what others are struggling with and I know how to overcome that barrier. I'm able to openly connect with others because I know the very feeling of being alone and isolated. I am able to connect because I know who I am. I know my identity. I know my weaknesses and I'm comfortable sharing that with others in a meaningful way. Once you've experienced the deep hurting of isolation, you do everything you can to connect with others who are experiencing that deep pain also. Once you've experienced authentic community, it's hard to settle for a counterfeit cultural expression of what community is.

We create community with the people we decide to invest our life with. I've spent years with people, and after that investment of time, I still had no community. I've also spent hours with people and felt a deep connection with them, like I've known them my entire life. I don't think it has much to do with time besides the fact that time leads to experiences, but it has much more to do with intentions and vulnerability. When you decide to let others in, to show others who you are, something remarkable happens. They often do the same thing.

It's difficult to have community if we don't know who we are as individuals. Knowing who we are as individuals takes intentionality and discipline through countless hours of introspection. Introspection is uncomfortable. It tells us in what ways we are lacking in character and mind. We like to pretend we have it all together all the time, but reality shows us that we don't have that many answers. Community assists us to find our identity and point us back to Jesus. But when that community is a bunch of dudes sitting uncomfortably around a circle mumbling about nothing, not a lot will change.

Community is often forged through difficult times or experiences that are shared with other individuals with a common goal. It's through action that community is formed—not just drinking coffee and acting like everything is okay. I've always found that action is the best catalyst for relationships imaginable. It's through action that we get to know others and find ourselves. Everyone is easy to get along with when it's smooth sailing. It's when things get rough that we truly learn who each other are.

Allow others' stories to collide with your own. Our stories are not meant to be isolated. Choose to fight together. We rely on God and others to move us along in our storyline. When we deny help from others, we deny them joy in life. Community is an intentional group of people coming together for the collective benefit of diversity and safety brought into the group by each member present. It should be a place that reflects everything that God is, a place where growth is natural, where we are pushed to become better people. Finding community is like coming home.

There's been a major switch in my perception of community over the past three years. My views on community have changed drastically. Before, I would have said I'm more of a lone-wolf type. I'm very comfortable alone. I'm very comfortable with myself and my thoughts. Most days it's easier for me to work on projects than it is to simply just hang with others. Projects give me a sense of meaning and accomplishment that is tangible. Coming to terms though, projects don't necessarily matter; it's people who matter. It's easier for me to get lost in the process or the project than to spend quality time with people. And maybe it's because I like control. With projects the results are almost all up to me. Relationships aren't like that. You can't control relationships; they are a living, growing thing. There's an ultimate risk with love. You don't know how people will react, but to put your heart out there is a dangerous thing. I've come to find that relationships are worth the investment and love is always worth the fight.

I've had a nasty habit of jumping from circle to circle, being involved in hundreds of things—all meaningful, all good things that I've been jumping from group to group to accomplish. I commonly get involved in numerous projects, finish those projects, and then jump ship to the next opportunity when it comes along. Until recently, I had no idea this circle hopping had to do more with commitment and vulnerability than my free, adventurous spirit. I didn't commit in part because when I was on the fringes, I didn't have to authentically connect since I was only involved in a short-term project. After completion I would seek out other opportunities and continue the cycle. The projects I was involved with were meaningful in various ways, but I was not truly known by those communities since I was jumping from group to group. I didn't connect because I was involved with everything. I wasn't rooted. My relationships were only as deep as the sixty minutes I could spare once a week. I found security in being involved in everything and vested in nothing. But that didn't give me the community my heart was desperately searching for. I wasn't known. I was holding back due to my own insecurities and fears. People didn't know that, but I knew that. I could feel the uneasiness within me.

What I've come to learn and appreciate is that humanity is fragile. We are more easily broken than we'd like to admit. We long for vulnerability but continue to hide amongst the shadows for fear that we are not enough. The sooner we realize this, the more we can connect in meaningful ways with ourselves, each other, and ultimately with God. Our prayers are answered by the sacrifices of others. It's remarkable how God works things out. God shows up in people. We are his representatives here on earth. You might say you've never seen God, but that's because you missed him working through those around you.

Don't miss out on what we're called to be a part of. I know a lot of people have been burnt by church and our connotations of what church is. But don't write it off completely; the church is simply a collection of people—broken people needing Jesus. Sometimes we get it right, and other times we don't. The church is a collection of followers of Jesus, regardless of denomination, coming together to celebrate the life we have been given through Jesus.

People will jump from community to community searching for the right people, for their own experience to match picture perfect with reality. That won't ever happen. Our realities and our experiences rarely align. You won't find perfect people anywhere, and you definitely won't find them in church. If they were perfect people, they wouldn't have any reason to be found in church. For wasn't it the great teacher himself who said, "It is not the healthy who need a doctor, but the sick" (Luke 5:31).

God works through people. I usually don't hear this thundering voice from the sky; I hear the voices of the people surrounding me daily. I hear the voices of my family, friends, and the occasional stranger speaking on behalf of God. I've seen the face of God on a number of occasions. The face of God looks like my mother, father, and brothers; it looks like humanity in action. God moves through people. People will show you a deeper side of God, for we are all reflections of his glory. We are the outpouring of his love, and our community brings heaven to earth. Authentic community with intentionality and vulnerability is the closest to heaven we will get on earth.

Don't miss out on community due to fear of being found out. That is what makes community beautiful—being found out and being loved in spite of your insecurities, flaws, and brokenness. How else will we connect with others unless we let them know us for who we are? Don't live your life as a second-rate someone else when you can be the one and only first-rate you. You are needed. All of you is needed.

Why relationships? You don't learn much about life, love, or God by living isolated, wandering around in the desert by yourself. You weren't made to. You were designed to live in community to reflect and gaze upon that reflection of God in others. Community is a pure reflection of the character of God. There are already too many actors and people wearing costumes. Wear your humanity on your sleeve. It's remarkable to see what happens when someone is raw, real, vulnerable and transparent. Walls come down. People connect. We find what we've been searching for—to be known, to be loved.

9 *288 SQUARE INCHES*

One of the many jobs I worked to help subsidize my university tuition was working as a weekend receptionist at a local nursing home facility in my hometown. I had some friends who had done it before me, and I knew the managers going into the whole experience. Overall, I stayed at that position for a little over a year and a half. We had good days and we had terrible days, but we mostly just had days. Things moved at a slower pace around that place.

There was always a manager on duty, supposedly, but since I was scheduled on the weekend, that meant there was actually no one in charge on the campus. Anytime anyone had a problem, I was the only one people were able to find. I cannot tell you how many problems I solved or people I sent away with answers to problems I didn't know existed. I wasn't given an overabundance of information on anything that we had at the facility. It was difficult to find the answers to all the questions people would ask, or to know the inner workings of the campus and all that would go on with each day. Every day I worked it seemed like the first day of the job.

One of the many lessons I learned from that job occurred while walking through the facility delivering the mail. I noticed outside the residents' rooms that there were these small shelves. Just normal everyday shelves with random small trinkets and a photo or two. They must have been nothing more than a 1 by 2 foot shelf—nothing major, nothing exciting that demands your attention, mainly just old-people things. But after walking those halls weekend after weekend, I realized those weren't just shelves; those were representations of the highlights from that person's life.

Their entire life was on display on one single tiny shelf outside their room. That was it. They had their life on display with 288 square inches.

We all start decomposing after a certain age. All of us are eventually going to die. We may feel invincible now, but after a while we'll start to realize that life is slipping out of our grasp. On this side of eternity we will die, our bodies will start to decay, and our earthly lives will come to an end. Death is part of the unofficial contract we signed at birth. This is a fact of life; we know that. Rarely, do we choose to dwell on the subject of death. We know our days on this earth will end. That's no surprise, but we don't live like we know it. We live like we'll be here for quite some time. We live our lives like we have a direct credit line that never faults, spitting out time like an ATM does cash. We live like we have an account of time that will never run dry.

When you come to the end of your life, make sure that what you display on your 288-square-inch shelf is worth it. Suddenly, money doesn't seem that important. The Porsche you've dreamed of driving isn't as shiny when it's only in a photograph. The time you traded with family in order to drive that car doesn't seem to compare to the time you missed out with your children any longer. Money isn't just money. Money represents actual hours of your life traded for compensation from a company or from a service you provided. Hours of your life are traded in for this resource; make the most of it. You only have so much room on your shelf; make sure that what you put on it is worth it to you. Life is short; count the cost of what you're building. The life we live, we live it day by day. Each day may not be that significant, but after you add those days together, they have the potential to become a meaningful story.

One of the most impactful things you could do today is to set aside time to focus on what you desire out of life. This is one of the most overlooked and underemphasized exercises one could do to clarify their own journey. Ask yourself, "What do I really desire out of life? What will truly satisfied me? What is my purpose?" If we don't take the time to formulate an answer to those questions, we will be running wild trying to find the answers in every direction possible. Life is hectic, and every opportunity isn't necessarily a good opportunity if it doesn't contribute to your ultimate life's story. It could be the perfect opportunity for someone else, but if it doesn't match up with your life's purpose, let it go. To accomplish a life worth living you need to be living for something worth dying for. You cannot be fully alive until you find something worth dying for. Find those things, your passions, and don't lose your focus to the thousands of distractions all around us demanding our attention.

God has given us a life to live. He's given us talents and abilities that are gifts to use for the betterment of all people. We have an opportunity to develop these gifts in order to be more influential, reaching people in numerous ways to build a kingdom based on love and redemption. God gives us the option to work toward something that is earthly or eternal. He actively lets us choose each and every day what kingdom we build. The materialistic things of this world will fade. We all know the things of this world will never satisfy, yet we don't live that way. Don't trade your life for things that will eventually lose value. Invest in what matters for eternity—invest in people.

We all have the ability to take God up on the adventure or to write our own story without the co-author. He gives us that choice. He also makes it clear that we will be accountable to what we choose to write with the days of our lives. Each day is a new blank page. The story is written by our lives day in and day out. Write a story worth telling your grandchildren about.

"Again, it will be like a man going on a journey, who called his servants and entrusted his wealth to them. To one he gave five bags of gold, to another two bags, and to another one bag, each according to his ability. Then he went on his journey. The man who had received five bags of gold went at once and put his money to work and gained five bags more. So also, the one with two bags of gold gained two more. But the man who had received one bag went off, dug a hole in the ground and hid his master's money.

After a long time the master of those servants returned and settled accounts with them. The man who had received five bags of gold brought the other five. 'Master,' he said, 'you entrusted me with five bags of gold. See, I have gained five more.' His master replied, 'Well done, good and faithful servant! You have been faithful with a few things; I will put you in charge of many

*things. Come and share your master's happiness!' The man with
two bags of gold also came. 'Master,' he said, 'you entrusted me
with two bags of gold; see, I have gained two more.' His master
replied, 'Well done, good and faithful servant! You have been
faithful with a few things; I will put you in charge of many
things. Come and share your master's happiness!' Then the
man who had received one bag of gold came. 'Master,' he said,
'I knew that you are a hard man, harvesting where you have
not sown and gathering where you have not scattered seed. So
I was afraid and went out and hid your gold in the ground. See,
here is what belongs to you.' His master replied, 'You wicked,
lazy servant! So you knew that I harvest where I have not sown
and gather where I have not scattered seed? Well then, you
should have put my money on deposit with the bankers, so that
when I returned I would have received it back with interest. So
take the bag of gold from him and give it to the one who has ten
bags. For whoever has will be given more, and they will have an
abundance. Whoever does not have, even what they have will
be taken from them. And throw that worthless servant outside,
into the darkness, where there will be weeping and gnashing of
teeth.'"*[1]

God has given all of us talents and abilities unique to us in
order to help those around us. It's a magnificent thing to have
the knowledge and ability to help those around us, to extend
a loving hand, giving freely because of Jesus' example. The resources God has provided for us were not our own to begin
with whether that is in the form of intellectual, social, profes-
sional, athletic, or any other skill set. He gave these resources

[1] Matthew 25:14-30

on loan. He's the ultimate investor; God provided the capital to get you going and on your feet; it's your business to make sure you use your abilities for God's glory. God has given you these gift and abilities and will help you develop them if you're willing. He doesn't just give them to you and leave you to get after it; he actively directs the growing process and prunes when necessary for our development and benefit. God is invested in you. He desires to see you succeed in the ways he has gifted you for his own benefit and glory.

I used to think this parable was harsh to the servant who was fearful and didn't invest the money. With any investment there is a certain degree of risk. The higher the degree of risk usually equates to a higher return or reward. My heart goes out to this guy, because if I'm being honest I could see myself doing the same thing. Many times I find that I'm scared to commit to things outside my comfort zone with thoughts flooding my head with inadequacy. It's a fearful thing to commit to something when you have no notion of the outcome. The thought that I could lose it all is enough to keep me stagnant.

Then I think about the other two guys, and I don't think that they were just fearless or reckless. I think they could see that the benefit outweighed the potential risk. I think they had a vision of what the return on investment could be, and they went after it. It's not that they didn't sense the risk of their involvement; it's that they could look beyond that risk and see that their master had entrusted them and believed in them to produce return from the initial capital investment. The master wanted them to succeed. This wasn't a huge test where the master expected them to fail. The master gave them something of value, believed in them, invested in them, and expected something vibrant to happen.

Using the gifts God has given you is one of the most fear-inducing things in the world. But wouldn't that make sense? Wouldn't Satan want to destroy the very things that God has specifically given to us to impact and change the world as only we can? Satan attacks us in those wounded places to keep us in check. All the while Jesus is slowly calling us to step out, throw off our insecurities and doubts, and place our faith not in ourselves and our abilities, but in him and his abilities.

Jesus calls us to more than we are. God has a vision of what we could be. He is actively molding us into something more, but that requires something from us. It requires us taking responsibility and risking our comfort. To find your talents, to find your passions, commonly means taking chances and seizing opportunities where the outcome is unknown. It means we'll mess up, fail, and do things wrong. And that's not the goal; it's just part of the process. It's time to do different things and do things differently. It's hard to realize your gifts and talents if you never leave the couch.

Maybe it's time we all swim out past our depth.

God doesn't just want his talents and abilities back; he desires tremendously more than that. When we use what God has given to us, our strengths and weaknesses, we grow closer to him in the process and closer to others because we realize we're in this together. We find a new resilience and motivation for the work God is doing all around us.

Going out into the wild is one of the most freeing feelings in the world. Only a few times in my life have I thought I was actually going to die in the wilderness—three times exactly. Those were the hardest experiences I've ever been through, but I've never felt more alive than during those moments of life or death. God will take you to the edge and push you further than you could imagine if you're willing to be used by him. You have to risk in order to grow. You can't grow if you're never stretched beyond what you've been before.

The same exists when I think about the moments God has brought me through spiritually. I've been in the deepest darkness and wandered through the driest desert for what seemed an eternity, only to find God was leading me in the exact direction I needed at that moment. I don't know why I had to go through those challenging experiences and why I still have to go through those dark, painful times. I really don't have a clear answer for that. But because I have this record of how God has proven himself numerous times to be faithful, I have more confidence and trust in the future battles we'll fight through side by side. I've heard it commonly referred to as the training ground—a place where we are prepared for what lies ahead, something bigger where the stakes are higher, something that would break me if I hadn't had these past experiences learning to depend exclusively on God. I'm not sure I'm ready for the next venture yet, knowing how intense the past trials have been, but I can only imagine what lies beyond the here and now.

Moses spent forty years in the desert before God told him he was ready to be used. He spent forty years with sheep in a desert. Not exactly my idea of effective time management on God's part. But God rarely operates in ways that we understand in the moment. It's not that the Israelites weren't enslaved that entire time because they were, but God was molding Moses into the leader his people needed. That takes time and experience to become a mature leader who would eventually be one of the most influential leaders in history.

My problem is that I want it instantly. I don't feel like I have forty years to wait. I want it now. Give me the big stuff, the heavy stuff, the things that matter. God continually states that I'm not ready for the heavy lifting just yet, and he also tells me the small things that I have been doing do, indeed, matter. Through these minor details and small accomplishments he's grooming me into the man who will do extraordinary things through his strength and for his kingdom, but it all takes time, bruises, mistakes, pain and small victories to mature into his ultimate vision of who I can become.

You are given the choice to use your abilities to further yourself or to further the Kingdom of God. He's given this choice for us to pursue daily. Some days I choose the winning side and some days I choose my own side. It's easy to get wrapped up in the day-to-day shuffle of things, forgetting my position as a son of the King and losing my perspective that this life is fleeting. I think about those shelves and it refreshes my memory to spend my life on what matters, not on which project to accomplish next. At the end of my life I hope I look back with a worn body, exhausted beyond measure, and overwhelmed by the gladness of the life God and I crafted together. Decide daily who you are going to serve, and the rest will take care of itself.

You have been given your talents, skills, and passions for a specific reason: to accomplish massive things for God's glory and plan of redemption. Don't waste your opportunity chasing after things that don't matter. When you choose to be someone else or chase someone else's passions, you rob others of what God designed for you to give away. Other people need you. This world needs you. Don't listen to the enemy and believe the lie that you are not essential, that you are worthless. You are more valuable than you could ever understand. Build your life on that foundation. Build your life on the value that Jesus gives you.

It's hard to live a story that matters. It requires a lot of sacrifice to chase down your dreams. It takes energy to live intentionally. It's not an easy thing to accomplish an effective and meaningful life. Is it worth it? More than you could imagine.

People are worth the investment. Love is worth the investment. Don't hold yourself back. Love recklessly. Don't trade this life for less than it's worth. The small choices we make compound into our life's story. Every day is a new white sheet of paper ready for the ink of your life to spill over the page. You only get 288 square inches; build something that matters.

10 DISCIPLINE BREEDS FREEDOM

I'm sure there has been plenty of speculation on whether one can actually live a life like Jesus, and sometimes I contemplate the same thing. The world we live in and the culture of our day and age are vastly changing every second, but what remains constant are human nature and, more importantly, the unfailing love of God. The more I dive in and study Scripture, getting my hands dirty doing the work of Jesus, I find again and again that what Jesus had to teach matches up exactly to life as it was intended to be lived. The truths and principles that Jesus lived out during his life here on earth transcend generations, cultures, countries, and people groups. God's principles are given to us as a guide, a standard of living, that will produce the most impactful, influential adventure we can fathom. If you think walking with God is boring, dull, or monotonous, I promise you haven't met him yet.

It's hard to imagine because the majority of people who say they believe the words of Jesus live in contrast to what God has shown and taught. But every now and then you meet someone who has truly experienced the love of Jesus—one of those people who live out what Jesus did, becoming his very hands and feet, a servant leader who is willing to leave everything he or she has known to chase the great mystery our hearts are longing for. We've just been too stubborn to admit that what Jesus has to say speaks into our lives, bringing fulfillment and joy we've never found elsewhere. I wholeheartedly believe Jesus came to bring us a world we've never imagined: "I have come that they may have life, and have it to the full" (John 10:10b).

I hope this book spurs you to pursue a life filled with the goodness and grace of Jesus Christ, helping you shine brightly in this dark and broken world. Our culture desperately needs people who are fearless to proclaim life to the lifeless, who are able to live with passion, to stand up for those who cannot stand for themselves. You are in a position to influence and change those around you in a certain way that no one else on the planet will ever be able to do exactly like you. You're unique and have been gifted with special abilities, strengths and weaknesses in order to relate to others in life-changing ways, sharing the redemption of Jesus.

God not only intended Scripture to teach us and show us the story of who he is, but he gave us the law to proclaim our freedom. James 2:12-13 says, "Speak and act as those who are going to be judged by the law that gives freedom, because judgment without mercy will be shown to anyone who has not been merciful. Mercy triumphs over judgment." The law gives freedom. It wasn't meant to hold us back from all the exciting things in life. It is in place to protect us and to protect our innocence and purity. Scripture is a guide to living the good life, the really good life, not just the empty pursuits of society. The longer I live the more I see this truth in all the lives around me and even in my own. It doesn't take long to see how abuse, divorce, unfaithfulness, lust, or drunkenness can readily ruin a life and a family. It's not to keep you from having fun; it's meant for you to find life—the very thing we were made for. The law gives freedom. Our discipline allows us to chase down whatever dream we desire to pursue.

At summer camp we always deliver the harsh rules on Sunday evening when the students arrive for the first time. I say harsh, but it's truly about five rules that are very basic and easy to follow; Listen to authority. Respect others. Be on time. Clean up after yourself. Have fun. Basically those are all the rules we have, and those are all the rules we ever want to have. The problem stems from students who try to bend the rules, who decide they're exempt from the rules, or who choose not to follow the simple rules that guide summer camp.

Personally, I hate rules. I hate enforcing the rules, and I always end up being the bad guy. I don't want rules. I would love camp to run without rules where the students were respectful and we could all have the time of our lives. Almost every time we give rules, the students abuse them, and we have to enforce and create more rules for the students to follow. These rules are not meant to be restrictive for the students; they are to give the students the best experience possible while keeping them safe and protecting other students at the same time. I'm convinced that I hate the rules more than the students do.

Rules aren't made to be restrictive; rules are made to ensure freedom is possible. With freedom comes responsibility, and someone, somewhere, has to sacrifice in order to make that possible. All the staff desire the students to have the best week of their lives, but to make that possible we have to lay the foundation of rules in the beginning to set the expectations of the week. Every single rule has a reason, and that reason is to produce the best camp experience. We didn't make rules for fun or to limit the camp experience. Rather, every rule has a meaning and leads to the best camp experience even when the students don't understand the need for certain rules. The students' understanding is limited in this environment; they haven't dealt with these issues before, but we have. We've been down this road once or twice and have seen the outcome of students with these same behaviors. We're desperately trying to protect them from unhealthy habits and devastating consequences.

Isn't that how it is with God?

God has given us these guidelines, commands, rules, and principles to guide us and protect us from even our own selfish desires. All the while he simply desires the best for us. He's trying to give us the best experience; he's trying to draw us in. He's been down this road once or twice before. In our limited understanding we believe we know what's best for our lives, and we forsake God, who is willing to selflessly show us the best things in life, what we're desperately searching for. We trade that experience for our inexperience and suffer the consequences.

We have a distorted view of God, one where he is holding out on us. We see him as an authority figure not letting us do what we want to do, throwing rules and regulations here and there to keep us in a box. Yet, he's entirely different than our false assumptions of who he is. God isn't holding out on us. The only thing that God is withholding from us is pain and brokenness from our own dark decisions and choices. That's it. God isn't withholding from you the good life; he's giving you the guide to the ultimate life.

It's heartbreaking sending a student home from camp.

You wish they would comprehend and understand the consequences of their actions. You wish they would understand that you have only their best interests in mind. We are selfless in the service toward these students, only wanting the best for them, but unfortunately some don't understand that.

Students buck the system and fight back against the rules. It's rare and painful to send a student home during a week of camp. We don't want to send any student home, but because they sometimes risk the integrity of camp, we have no other choice.

I want to enjoy camp more than most campers want to enjoy camp. I think it's the same with God. We have this wrong idea that he is this righteous, angry figure, ready to pronounce judgment on anyone who's not perfect. It's not that he isn't perfectly just; he is, but he is so much more. He's inviting us to play a vital role with him as our guide and ultimate companion. He doesn't like rules. Jesus broke most of the rules of his day and age. It seems like most of the stories in the Gospels are instigated or followed by Jesus rebelling or not following the standards of that day set in place by man.

When students pull you aside and say, "Thank you. That was the best week of my life. I can't wait to be here next year," it's the best part of the whole camp experience. That makes all the sacrifices and long days worth it. Can you imagine what God feels like if we would come to the end of our time here on earth and be like, "That was insane. What an incredible life. Thanks for that, God. Thanks for making that happen. Thanks for writing my story"?

This is a miniscule example of what God has entrusted to us, but we don't have that many rules either. Love God. Love people. God has given us guidelines to follow in order for us to live a better life. That's exactly what happens when we choose to pursue life under God's guidelines: we find what it means to truly be alive. Life happens when we follow after God's heart and the passions and gifts that God has entrusted to us. To leave your heart behind would be a vital mistake.

This is what David said in Psalm 1:

> *Blessed is the one*
> *who does not walk in step with the wicked*
> *or stand in the way that sinners take*
> *or sit in the company of mockers,*
> *but whose delight is in the law of the LORD,*
> *and who meditates on his law day and night.*
> *That person is like a tree planted by streams of water,*
> *which yields its fruit in season*
> *and whose leaf does not wither—*
> *whatever they do prospers.*
>
> *Not so the wicked!*
> *They are like chaff*
> *that the wind blows away.*
>
> *Therefore the wicked will not stand in the judgment,*
> *nor sinners in the assembly of the righteous.*
> *For the LORD watches over the way of the righteous,*
> *but the way of the wicked leads to destruction.*

What David talks about is a disciplined life. As a society, we despise the word *discipline*. We associate discipline with a rather lame, hard, or uneventful life. The truth about discipline in any sector of life is that at the root of discipline we find freedom. Discipline breeds freedom. Discipline provides the means necessary to rise above our current circumstances and forge a path of change. The guidelines God lays out for our lives aren't made to dull our senses or keep us tame; they are made for our benefit and to make us more alive than ever before. The Jews and the Romans didn't crucify Jesus because he was boring. Jesus was crucified because he was dangerous and a threat to the system.

Living our lives with discipline will enable numerous opportunities for us to serve and to love others. God honors the small things and will entrust us with more influential opportunities as the time arises. By living life with God's principles in mind, we are in harmony with God and what he is masterfully creating.

I believe God gives us more opportunities to come alive and find a deeper understanding of who he is when we live lives of godly discipline and reckless abandonment. Discipline doesn't mean living boring lives; it's quite the opposite actually. When we follow God's guidelines, we come alive and everything radically changes.

In my experience big things build on the small things done faithfully. God didn't just drop massive opportunities in my lap without the continuous, small, challenging opportunities that he gave me to build my integrity and character. For me the momentum is only growing, and it has all come by living faithfully and abiding by God's guidelines. That's not to say that I haven't jacked things up and made a thousand mistakes or the same mistakes a thousand times, but God's grace is enough. He restores and sees me through the blood and redemption of Jesus.

This brings us to a place where God can use us in the midst

of daily life, which is a powerful thing. We underestimate how much God uses the small, everyday situations to impact the world. I used to think changing the world meant I had to write a book, start a non-profit, move to a third world country and pass out vaccines to those without access to healthcare, but that's not what changing the world is. Changing the world is as simple as befriending someone who is lonely, smiling at a passing stranger, listening to someone's story, being a mentor to a kid who has no one to look up to, and many more ideas that have yet to be thought of. The best definition of love I've ever heard is as simple as this, "See a need; meet a need." We change the world through small, everyday interactions with others.

Don't discount yourself because you're not the CEO of a major corporation. Life isn't about that. Use the time and resources that you have to reach those hurting around you. God doesn't ask you to use what he didn't give you. He asks you to team up with him using what he designed you to do. God desires to leverage the passions that he gave you, not what he gave someone else. You don't have to look far to see the brokenness. If you wait until you can do everything for everyone, you'll miss the opportunity to do something for someone. You always have something left to give. No matter where your feet wander, God can always use you if you are willing. God always gives us that choice.

Life isn't worth living when we live for ourselves. When we lose our heavenly perspective, life becomes frustrating, hard, and largely, pointless. We see all trials and hardships as a burden to survive instead of a divine opportunity to grow and develop into the character God has planned for us to play. Jesus invites us into something meaningful and dangerous. If you truly want your life to matter, you won't back down from doing the hard things because you will understand the only meaningful outcomes come by love and sacrifice. We can only willingly sacrifice ourselves if we know the one who sacrificed himself for us even when we were beyond grace, deemed worthless. I don't think it was an easy task for Jesus either, but he counted the cost and decided you and I were worth it.

Jesus proclaimed in Luke 9:23-25, "Then he said to them all: 'Whoever wants to be my disciple must deny themselves and take up their cross daily and follow me. For whoever wants to save their life will lose it, but whoever loses their life for me will save it. What good is it for someone to gain the whole world, and yet lose or forfeit their very self?'"

Life is what we are desperately searching for. Subconsciously, I continue to blame God for holding out on me with things that I believe would increase my life experience. All the while God knows these futile things will harm me and not bring the life I desire. Numerous times I've asked, "God, this is the perfect opportunity, the perfect relationship, or the perfect job. Why would you say no to something this good?" And deep down I feel like God is holding out on me, that he's holding back things that I deserve and desire in life.

These tough situations lead me to ask the question, "Is it for my benefit?" I don't know. I hope so. But what I do know, and what Scripture tells us time after time, is that it is for God's glory. If I believe those verses, that should be enough to convince me to live for that reason alone even when things don't go my way, even if it feels like God is holding out on me.

Time after time I start to believe the lies of society that I am missing out, that God is holding out on the good life for me.

That by living my life on God's terms I am missing out on the best things this world has to offer. I consume that lie over and over again, and like any propaganda, I start to believe it after a while. It's only then that I trade the promises of God for the broken and shallow things of this world to realize that it cannot fulfill the empty promises that it boasted of. I thought these accomplishments, relationships, finances, and possessions would bring life, but they just left me emptier than before.

Life isn't as hard to live as we make it out to be. You don't have to read thousands of books to understand how to live life successfully. There aren't 7 magic steps to a better, more fulfilling life. It's all about Jesus. Life is about pursuing God and doing what you love. Don't make it more complicated than it needs to be. Rules aren't meant to be restrictive, and what God commands is for our benefit and freedom. Don't think God is holding out or you're missing out on life if you're a follower of Jesus. There isn't anything else more worthwhile in all of life.

When we operate our lives outside of God's rules we end up broken, scarred, and damaged. Our own quest for freedom brings bondage. Walking in full obedience to God is true freedom. God writes these principles to guide our lives, to give us the ultimate source of life—himself. Obedience enables his power in our lives:

> *Therefore, since we are surrounded by such a great cloud of witnesses, let us throw off everything that hinders and the sin that so easily entangles. And let us run with perseverance the race marked out for us, fixing our eyes on Jesus, the pioneer and perfecter of faith. For the joy set before him he endured the cross, scorning its shame, and sat down at the right hand of the*

throne of God. Consider him who endured such opposition from sinners, so that you will not grow weary and lose heart.[1]

To take this one step further, our lives shouldn't just be about staying within the lines and tip-toeing around, trying to avoid reprimand. We shouldn't only try to avoid the bad things and follow all the rules to a T, but we should conduct our lives by solely pursuing things that catapult us forward to knowing God in a deeper way—not simply avoiding the bad, but focusing in on the ultimate way to live. Is what we are doing with our most valuable resources not only avoiding the bad, but is it impacting our pursuit of God in the most beneficial way? Are we radically committed to pursue glorifying God at any cost?

---

[1] Hebrews 12:1-3

11 THERE SHOULD BE A DIFFERENCE

Here a great number of disabled people used to lie—the blind, the lame, the paralyzed. One who was there had been an invalid for thirty-eight years. When Jesus saw him lying there and learned that he had been in this condition for a long time, he asked him, "Do you want to get well?"[1]

I always found it puzzling why Jesus, who we believe knows all things, would ask this paralyzed man what he desires. I also love the rawness of the Bible. It calls this man just as society did, "invalid." He's not invalid in the eyes of God, but he's invalid in the eyes of his society. Isn't the answer obvious? This man wants to be healed, to be made well. This invalid man wants to become someone who matters in society. Isn't that something we all crave? Deep within we all have the longing to know we contribute, to know our story matters.

That's always what I thought at least. Clearly, if I were this man, I would want Jesus to heal me, to make me whole, to validate my situation in life. To be healed would mean a world of

[1] John 5:3-6

difference; it would open up numerous opportunities. This is what this man has been desperately wanting all of his life.

But with all these new opportunities also come new responsibilities. This man would now have to work for his wages; he would have to provide for himself and validate his own situation. He would never be at the grace and the charity of the city's people anymore. He would have to forge his own path. He would have to take responsibility for his situation.

With this man, as with our current condition in our culture, he was terrified of forging his own path—afraid of stepping out, afraid of making mistakes, and stagnant out of fear. It's one thing to know God's will; it's entirely another thing to live that out. One of my mentors recently asked me two questions. The first question he asked me was, "What do you feel like God is calling you toward?" And the second question was similar, "What are you going to do about it?" Make no mistake the second answer is as equally important as the first.

God was pointing the invalid man to something bigger. It's not only that Jesus has the ability and power to make this man whole again on a physical level; Jesus has the authority to make him complete on all levels. I think that's what Jesus was showing us through this encounter—the bigger picture. Jesus never disregards our current circumstances, big or small; he cares about the minute details, but he always points us to something bigger.

What if God already knew the darkness of the human heart and the human condition? The lesson I learned over a year ago, while working in the emergency department, is that people don't always want to get better. Some people are complacent with the way things are. They are content with not doing the necessary footwork to accomplish what needs to be done or the effort to put their dreams into action. People may talk as if they want to do something or accomplish something, but reality often proves otherwise.

This is an encounter I had with my first patient who refused treatment, who refused to get better.

Looking into his eyes I could see the pain that has marked this man's entire life, but there was no way I was able to help him. I reached out my arm, but I can only bear so much weight before I have to let go. I couldn't save him. He was younger than my dad, and he was going to die.

He had a chance to live, a good chance, to live twenty more years, and he walked away from what could save him, the treatment that could likely cure him. It's his right to refuse treatment—against medical advice—but I didn't think I'd actually witness him walk out of the emergency department that night never to come back.

He said he didn't want treatment. He didn't want to get better. He was ready to go home and slowly die, alone.

We gave him all the relevant information and told him the consequences; we even had a room set up for him to start treatment that same night at the hospital. It's not an unfamiliar prognosis and it comes with a good outcome, but he still chose to walk away. We gave him alternative options about outpatient treatment and told him to come back anytime if we could help in any way possible. But he won't be back. He'll never walk through those hospital doors again.

It's a sad reality that life can be so difficult that you're not willing to fight anymore, that society pushed you into the darkness, and you found yourself broken and alone. My heart breaks over people who refuse to get better, who refuse to change, who remain stagnant due to lack of courage and value.

Unfortunately it happens all too often. People end their lives, give up the fight, or refuse treatment for healing day in and day out. They don't realize the value they have. They don't know the value of their identity, the value that God has placed on their lives.

We give value to the things we buy because of what we use to purchase that item with. An object is assigned value by the one who purchases it. You're worth what you were purchased for. God bought you with the perfect, spotless blood of Jesus Christ. You have value. You have meaning. Don't let anyone tell you otherwise.

Where does that leave us? I'd say it's a rare person who desires change passionately enough to pursue it wholeheartedly. Jesus gives us a valuable picture of what that life looks like, and it's not as romantic or glorified as we disillusion ourselves into thinking. When we want to get better, we have to change. Without intentional change and discipline, there will be no progress. It's not much different than other aspects of our lives, such as athletics, academia, relationships, and various goals we have. If you want to improve, you have to put in the effort. You don't become an Olympic athlete just by sitting around thinking about it. You dedicate your life to that dream. Those are the people we watch on TV, the same ones who wake at 4 a.m. to start their training every single day.

Not everyone's story has to end with them walking out of the emergency department, refusing treatment. People are being made new daily. God has the ability to change the heart of mankind. It's not an easy process as some have learned; it is at times painful and full of hardships, but it will produce the most meaningful life possible. I don't believe anything else in life compares to the beauty that God can create out of a broken life.

Take, for example, my new friend Carlos. Rushing through the haze of a busy life, I often forget at times other people around me who have a similar story to my own. They have battles they're fighting, demons that haunt them, and wars they've already won. When we take off our masks, I find that their stories and my story aren't that different.

I met Carlos when I was downtown shooting photos of the Cincinnati skyline. I love the city at night, so I was trying to capture the mood surrounding the environment. I was especially drawn to the courthouse, sitting in the middle of downtown, radiating justice and truth in a city full of brokenness. It's in a section in downtown with a rough crowd loitering on the steps and intimidating those brave enough to walk across that path. As I'm fumbling around with the shutter speed, ISO, and any other button I can manage to press on my camera, this man approaches me, and slightly jokingly, asks me to take his picture in front of the courthouse. Laughing, a very nervous laugh, I said sure. He asked if I'd put it in the paper believing me to be a reporter, and I said, "Not this time, my friend."

But he did ask me what I would say about him, what his caption would be.

That question made me think deeply about what I would have assigned to him as his caption before I asked him what he would say about himself. I might have just titled it, "Another Homeless Encounter" or something along those lines. But when I asked him what he would say about himself if he could write the caption, he replied without hesitation, "Bad Man Turned Good." I inquired further and he told me, "I used to be locked up in this county jail many nights, but I got tired of being the bad guy. I changed. Now I don't do anything to anybody that I wouldn't want them to do to me."

Maybe he's not just another homeless man. Quite possibly, he's just a product of his environment and upbringing that trapped him in the system, fighting to break free. Not every person is the same, not every person has the same background even though they can come from similar situations. Don't write people off just because you've met someone like them before. There should be a difference in how we treat others because God has placed value on every single human life. The image of God is ingrained in each one of us. Sometimes you just have to dig deep enough to find it. You have to step down from a place of judgment to the level of love, get your hands dirty, and love people where they are.

Never write someone out of the books without giving them a chance. Even after they blow that chance, don't write them out of the books. God didn't treat us that way. We all have stories. Some of those stories we can never explain, and some we can never forget, but our experiences inevitably shape who we are. Everyone has a story; we collectively need to start listening instead of being solely focused on writing our own story.

Bad man turned good. It's never too late to change. It's impossible to brush shoulders with Jesus and not be changed. That's the power of God. He changes us. From death and darkness on the inside to something more, to life and light. He brings love out of the fear. Isn't that true of all our stories? Bad man turned good by the grace of Jesus. God is in the business of redemption, and it's never too late to change.

Two things are needed for purposeful change to occur. The first is to come to a place of understanding by asking, "Are we are okay? Do we need change?" The second is similar: "Am I willing to do what it takes to change?" No noticeable change will take place until we can answer these questions with honesty. You will never grow if you are not willing to change.

We need to be able to come to a place where we can articulate that we are in fact not all right. We are broken, and we are wounded. From that place of vulnerability, we will begin to desire a change from the circumstances we're in. That's where and when the difference takes place. If we never come to a state that we need Jesus, there's not a whole lot of ground to go off of. Jesus came to seek and save those who are lost. Jesus states this clearly in Matthew 9:12-13, saying, "It is not the healthy who need a doctor, but the sick. But go and learn what this means: 'I desire mercy, not sacrifice.' For I have not come to call the righteous, but sinners." When we come to realize our need for Jesus and begin to accept that need, that is when change will start to occur in our lives. Until that moment of vulnerability, nothing meaningful can happen.

One of the greatest things in life is knowing when you go through certain life experiences you come out the other side a different person. Tough situations produce change in our lives. Every natural thing God created was designed for change. Humanity is no exception. In a good story the characters always have to face various trials to overcome in order to be transformed into the hero the story needs. This is called the character arc. If the character doesn't face a challenge or isn't changed in the process, you will lose interest in the story within minutes. A plot where the character doesn't change is a terribly boring story.

The same principle applies when you experience God. God is continuously challenging us by placing us in the uncomfortable in order to grow us as people. The character arc isn't an enjoyable concept when you're in the middle of it. Realize, though, that without trials and hardships nothing meaningful in life would develop. There would be no difference.

People should be able to tell there is a difference by the way we live our lives. If we claim to follow Jesus, and people are not able to discern a difference in our lives from society, we need to reassess our situation. When people genuinely encounter Jesus, they are changed. No one has ever encountered Jesus and stayed the same. When we experience life, God changes us in the process. With the correct perspective we can actively choose to grow better because of the situations God leads us through or we can choose to remain the same.

Influence is a powerful thing. Change occurs from the multiple sources that influence us. Research has exposed that the three biggest influences in our lives include the crowd we hang with, the books we read, and the movies we watch. These three influences are the driving factors of our lives. The good thing is, we have the ability and responsibility to decide how these three major influences will impact us. We become the people we spend our time with, the books we read, and the movies we watch. Choose wisely. If we desire a different outcome, we will have to intentionally make changes in our daily routine.

Change happens daily. We grow into who our parents are,

who our teachers are, and whom society prescribes us to be. It has to be a conscious decision on our part if we desire to be someone different than the crowd mentality, different than what society is grooming us toward. To be different we will have to stand out from the crowd, and we will have to swim upstream if we choose to follow what Jesus has called us toward.

God has a life planned for you that will require everything of you. You cannot be half in and half out, doing your own thing and doing God's thing. You have to be willing to take the risk to let go of what is known to venture into the great unknown. This life will take everything out of you. You have to go into every day prepared to give it your all. Being different and expecting more out of life will leave you exhausted.

Jesus called us to this lifestyle multiple times by broadcasting, "If anyone would come after me, let him deny himself and take up his cross and follow me" (Matthew 16:24). This is one of the most difficult things in life, to humble ourselves daily. The transformation of becoming selfless instead of pursuing selfish ambition as the world tempts us toward takes enormous amounts of energy to counteract in order to love like Jesus. We become effective followers of Jesus when we start doing what Jesus did—loving people, loving people who our society declares not deserving of our love or attention. The people around Jesus ridiculed him since he chose to surround himself with those of low position, those who held no value in society. He wasn't afraid of his reputation being stained or marred, for he knew the true value of people. People are always worth the investment. Love is always worth the fight.

You become different because you are now a new creation when your identity is rooted in who God says you are. You have been given a new identity in Jesus. You are not the same as you once were. God has taken the heart of stone and replaced it with a heart of flesh. Our lives become different on the outside because of the transformation within. If we start with the outside and don't produce change on the inside, eventually we will burn out and revert back to old habits. We get tired of hearing the phrase "from the inside out," but that is exactly how meaningful change works. If we don't value ourselves, we will never make the changes necessary to better ourselves. The results will never be enough to offset the sacrifice unless we take Jesus at his word and believe that we have value.

Jesus came to redeem our lives and bring us back from the realm of darkness to the kingdom of light. He calls us sons and daughters. We are equal and of the same heavenly lineage because he has adopted us into his family, calling us his own. God has chosen us. God desires us. God has given us value.

In the book of Acts, which talks about the events that occurred after Jesus defeats death and the start of the Church, chapter 4 states, "When they saw the courage of Peter and John and realized that they were unschooled, ordinary men, they were astonished and they took note that these men had been with Jesus." People could see that these men had been in the presence of Jesus, and they were changed because of it. They weren't afraid to live out their new identity in Jesus; they had been changed. The core of who they were was made new, and the people noticed.

This verse comes at the crucial point in the history of the world. Peter and John were under fire from the religious leaders of the day for healing and proclaiming life and salvation in the name of Jesus Christ. Even though these people wanted to shut them up and also didn't believe what they were preaching, they couldn't help but take notice that these men had been with Jesus. These ordinary men were changed by the presence of Jesus Christ, the man from Nazareth.

People aren't going to know unless someone tells them. People are climbing trees in order to see Jesus; and we're standing on the sidelines in silence. If you came to faith in Jesus, someone had to tell you. If you believe, someone had to introduce you in the first place. God called us to make disciples and to love people. Those are two incredibly difficult things. Those could be the two hardest things you will ever do in your life. It's not easy. You will fail, you will fall, you will get bruises, and you will lose some blood along the way. But in the end all of the struggle will be worth it. It will be worth all the pain, the rejection, and the humiliation when we see the open loving arms of our Father.

You cannot rub shoulders with Jesus and not be changed.

I desire that radical change; I desire to be so consumed by God that people can see his presence in my daily life. There's nothing more I desire in life than for others to see the light within me and praise God in heaven who made it all possible. The longer I live, the more I realize that Jesus is the only thing that matters. Everything else is meaningless. If it isn't about Jesus, I don't want to be part of it.

If you desire to become different, let Jesus validate your life. I guarantee you'll stand apart from the crowd. When you live a life like that, your entire outlook on life will be flipped; your perspective cannot remain the same. To be different you have to live differently. You need a new identity; your core needs to be changed before anything of substance is produced. Start reading the Bible for yourself and dig into what Jesus is about. Replicate that. Don't replicate what other Christians are saying and doing; replicate what Jesus is saying and doing. Don't follow people. Follow Jesus.

12 STORIES WORTH TELLING

Living life for any amount of time you may have reached the conclusion that life can be hard, challenging, and sometimes brutal. Living a life like Jesus is no different. All of our problems don't suddenly fall away. Jesus himself, we often find, experienced the same challenging things throughout his time on earth. If his life is any indication of what ours should reflect, we need to gear up in order to be ready for the hurdles coming our way.

There are many times in life that I ask, "How does Jesus do this?" In fact that's almost a daily question. How does Jesus love in such a selfless and relentless way when sometimes it's hard for me to find the strength to smile at others, let alone love them deeply?

Loving people is hard work. It's the most difficult and the most important thing in life. Perhaps that is exactly why we're not that good at it. It's exhausting. It takes everything from us. It's completely against our fallen human nature, and I think Satan plays to that element.

There were a lot of mundane and ordinary interactions between Jesus and his disciples, yet he never wasted an opportunity to teach, encourage, or pour life into those he was surrounded by. He sought out those opportunities and loved passionately through any and all circumstances. It wasn't just straight miracles all the time. It was a lot of hot, sweaty walking to and fro. The small glimpse of what we have in the Gospels is miniscule in the totality of what Jesus accomplished with his time on earth.

We fall into this misconception that if we are following God and are going about his business, things will fall into place and everything will work smoothly. I think that's absurd. How did that go for the disciples? The very ones closest to Jesus, who walked and talked with him for three years, what outcome did following Jesus produce in their lives here on earth? In the Scriptures we find that two of the disciples were martyred, and one was exiled to the island of Patmos. History would reveal that the other disciples were martyred, stoned, burned alive, stabbed to death, or crucified. I have trouble finding the disciples sitting around talking about how to live their best life now, ten steps to becoming a better man, or reaching your highest level of success. Society has distorted what following Christ truly means.

Our culture has produced this easy, laid-back Christianity where if it's meant to be it'll be, and if not, then don't worry about it. They say if it's hard or unimaginable than it's clearly not God's will. They also suggest, "Yeah, Jesus did that. But I'm not Jesus; I can't do that." And so we find ourselves in the midst of Christians who aren't truly desiring transformation or intentionally living to become more like Jesus, and that's a problem. We clump life into sections where Jesus can be involved, and other sections where he's not invited along. Life shouldn't be compartmentalized like that. A life following after

Jesus shouldn't be lived like that. When it is, we simply settle for mundane, and we slide into conformity with the norm.

God can and will call us to pursue hard things and that's okay. It's beneficial to us for growth, taking us deeper in our faith and understanding of who God is and what he is about. Simply because it's hard doesn't mean it's not meant to be. We have to let go of the mentality that everything meaningful is easy. It's not. Those challenges that we face end up shaping who we become. Growth rarely comes from the smooth times in life.

I'm not saying this to dissuade you or to tell you that it's always hard, or lonely, or isolating, because it's not. That's a small majority of life, the part of life marred by sin. Jesus desires the complete opposite of those things. Often, our battles are fought on the upsides of mountains. We're stepping on dangerous territory anytime we go against the grain. Anytime we choose love over hate, or perhaps love over indifference, we will face countless obstacles impeding us. Love is what will change the world.

Not only is it hard to love, but there's a lot in this life that actively distracts us from achieving what matters. It's an endless pit that we subconsciously fall into. There will always be boundless distractions to keep us from living a story worth telling. Living a story with meaning isn't easy, and it comes at a price. There's always a price to pay for living your life differently.

Often, I find that I'm out of sync when I'm placed in a conversation about current sporting stats or the latest news in pop culture. I don't follow those things. I realize I only have so much mental capacity to store information and a limited amount of energy to expend on learning. I pick and choose that which is most important to me and let go of things that don't produce real meaning in my own life—mainly sports and pop culture.

The payoff is that I've seen phenomenal results because of the lifestyle I've chosen and the decisions I've made. It far outweighs knowing the latest stats in baseball or the hottest celebrities in the media. It has no real bearing on my life. Controlling my thoughts and decisions has real impact. Choosing to think and dwell on things of substance produces real results in my life. That takes intentionality and mental focus to actively say no to other opportunities in order to have the resources to do what matters.

The older I get, the more I realize I can't do everything. Time is proving how true that is. If we become more intentional, we can chisel away the things in our lives that don't produce the outcomes we desire and spend our resources on things that do.

This comes about with a decision to simplify life. I was living the lie that being busy translated to being ultra-spiritual or important. But that wasn't the truth. I was so busy doing good things that I was missing out on what God was actually calling me toward. I was killing myself, running from thing to thing without time to rest or time for community. God doesn't require the world out of us; neither should we expect it from ourselves. It's easy to type these words, but the truth is that I'm writing this between running from thing to thing. I'm distracted most days and lose sight of what ultimately matters—Jesus. Everything else is just wasted ambition without God. We live in a culture where busy is the new normal, but that isn't necessarily what God is telling us to pursue. We are all so exhausted from rushing around being busy that we aren't actually being effective.

Get away and spend time piercing the surface of what we are doing and the why behind our activities. We are by nature creatures of habit and creatures of a herd mentality. Just because someone else is doing something, that doesn't mean that is what we are all supposed to be doing. Be intentional with everything you're involved with, whether that is people, activities, organizations or personal time. Make it count toward a higher purpose.

When sowing a garden, you only have so many nutrients in the soil and space to utilize to plant whatever you choose to grow. As your seedlings grow, you need to thin them, cut out even some of the good plants, in order for others to make it successfully because the soil might not be able to sustain them all. It seems weird to kill good plants, the very results you are trying to achieve, but if you leave them growing along with the others, all the plants will eventually die.

Knowing when and how to thin seedlings is vital for overall health and success. Thinning of plants allows the remaining plants growing room to receive all the growing requirements—adequate moisture, nutrition, good air circulation, and light—without having to compete with the other plants. Gosh, this sounds so familiar. I have a terrible time thinning things from my life. All these random activities and distractions take away from the growth I so desperately desire to see in my life. I keep running and running while I simply just need to thin the plants in my garden.

There's a phrase that has stuck with me over the past eight months and that is "Keep the first thing first." It has helped to prioritize my life when things seem out of control. Constantly, I need reminders of what my goals are and which ones require my immediate energy the most. I quit everything that is non-essential and start focusing my energy on things that are most impactful and influential in my life and others.

Am I still busy? Yes, I don't think that will ever change. But now I am doing things that truly make a difference in tangible, everyday ways. Life is much more fulfilling and bursting with vigor. A lot of life changes when we become intentional with our purposes and actions.

Don't waste any more of your time comparing yourself to others around you. The act of comparison won't get you far in life, except where you started. When we compare ourselves with others, we are actively placing chains on our hands and feet, which deliberately hold us back from the potential that God created us to have. He calls us each to a different journey. The time we waste comparing our lives to those around us we will never get back. We all have a different path in front of us. The only path worth traveling is the one God has laid in front of you. Don't turn to the left or to the right. Stay focused on the life God has called you to live even when it differs from the norm, especially when it differs from the norm.

If God calls you to be something, then decide that you will be the best possible version of what God has designed you to be. Don't look around at everyone else and wonder why God chose you for the task he did. Accept what God has designed for you and decide to make your life about God's purposes and for his story.

Jesus said, "Feed my sheep. Very truly I tell you, when you were younger you dressed yourself and went where you wanted; but when you are old you will stretch out your hands, and someone else will dress you and lead you where you do not want to go." Jesus said this to indicate the kind of death by which Peter would glorify God. Then he said to him, "Follow me!"

Peter turned and saw that the disciple whom Jesus loved was following them. (This was the one who had leaned back against Jesus at the supper and had said, "Lord, who is going to betray you?") When Peter saw him, he asked, "Lord, what about him?"

Jesus answered, "If I want him to remain alive until I return, what is that to you? You must follow me."[1]

Jesus called Peter to something more fulfilling than the life of a fisherman. Jesus takes Peter's life and uses him to build the foundation of his church. The life of a common, everyday man was transformed by the power of Jesus. Peter was the founding father of the church.

Peter asked what would happen to John, and Jesus only redirects his focus back to the task at hand. You have to choose who you are going to follow. You have to choose your focus.

John had his story, and Peter had his own. They were equally important, but they couldn't be reversed. God had called them to their own purpose, ultimately for God's purpose. Don't be consumed by the lives of others. Be focused on living a life worthy of the gospel of Jesus. When we compare our stories with others, we end up broken, in competition, and lost, trying to exceed each other. Jesus shows us another way is possible.

---

[1] John 21:18-22

It's astonishing how God uses the pain we experience to bring us to a place of redemption. Yet when I look back over my life, I find that God has done significant work and has torn my chest wide open, placing my heart in his hands and patching the holes inside. He took the shattered pieces and made something stunningly beautiful and will continue to do so until the day I breathe my last. The pain I experienced, the weight that was so crushing, was only temporary compared to the restoration God has accomplished in my life.

When you know your value, you don't let others dictate who you are or who you should be. You are valuable because you are loved and chosen by God. Your value isn't dictated by the changing opinions of others or society, the work you do, the amount of money you make, the relationships you have or the things you accomplish in life. You have intricate value because God placed his hands over you and formed your very being; he designed you perfectly with all your flaws and failures to be the only person on this planet who can do what you do. It's now your job to figure out what you bring to life that no one else does and then go and live that.

Two questions that have been lingering in my mind and shaping my life recently are:

1. What do I want out of life?
2. What can I offer the world no one else can?

These two questions may take some time to answer properly. I'm not quite sure I could give you a good answer for either of them at the moment. I think I'm finally growing into both questions and discovering the intersection of where they merge. When you can answer both of those questions and find the intersection, it's one of the most fulfilling spots in life. Through searching for the answers intrinsically, I have found value in seeing the differences I bring to the world that are unique to myself. That has made all the difference.

What do I want out of life? Gosh, a lot. More than my time on earth will allow. If I could reduce it all to one thing, I would say to show others that there is a better story worth telling. When all is stripped away, I desire my life to reflect God's love in every aspect.

Never forget your value stems from God's love and abundance in your life—nothing else. Everything will fade in the end; everything else is meaningless.

Love isn't as confusing as we make it out to be. You don't need to read more books on the subject. You can stop going to conferences, and TED Talks won't help you love better. All you really have to do is care. You have to care enough to take action, to reach out, to go where you are needed. When you see a need, you meet that need. You don't need to wait for permission. You don't have to wait on an answered prayer from God. You don't have to ask; you just do it. God has prepared this moment for you. You are here at this very place and time for a specific reason. You were called to do this. Indifference leads to an insignificant life. Choose to love. Choose to be broken for others.

God's grace abounds in the cracks and depravity of my soul. It's in my weakness that his love shines through the most. Faith manifests itself when we come to the end of who we are. It's in those moments that we are able to see if what we say we believe and what we actually believe align. This verse is a crux in my life. "But he said to me, 'My grace is sufficient for you, for my power is made perfect in weakness.' Therefore I will boast all the more gladly about my weaknesses, so that Christ's power may rest on me" (2 Corinthians 12:9).

I've struggled with grace most of my life. It's an everyday struggle to choose God's grace or work hopelessly toward my own saving grace. I hate failure. I'm driven to succeed in order to be found worthy and accepted by others. I desire to prove that I am good enough on my own, that I can save myself. It leaves me empty, exhausted, and alone.

God made a way. He carved a river through the desert and brought life to what once was dead. I would never be enough to save myself, and God was already aware of that fact. To my surprise, he was overwhelmingly alright with that.

God has always been telling me that I am good enough. Whispering that truth through the people he's placed in my life, through his Spirit, and through the words he's given to me. I simply couldn't believe him or take him at his word. It's hard to let go of flaws, expectations, and failures and openly trade those for freedom. There is freedom when you can let go of the weight that crushes mind, body and spirit.

I don't have to hide my brokenness or boast in my strengths any longer. I can simply be who I am, knowing that God has told me I am good enough. God has only ever wanted my freedom and had the best in mind for me. He paid the price of life for my life, freely giving me all things. Second chances are what God's heart is all about.

Because of Jesus ordinary people are empowered by extraordinary presence. Be an everyday hero. We don't need any more superheroes; we just need people who live with abandonment who are passionately following after Jesus.

We don't need more self-help books; we need more of Jesus. We've been kidding ourselves to think that if we follow seven principles, our lives will turn out phenomenally. Rules don't work; love does. Jesus shows us how to love more deeply and freely and that's what makes the difference. Without Jesus this whole life falls apart. It's useless. I don't want any more rules or bullet points; I desire to see God's heart.

Because of Jesus:

I can be myself.

I don't fear failure.

I can risk my life.

I can laugh at myself.

I can be wrong.

I don't have to be perfect.

I can lose and be happy.

I don't have to have my future figured out.

I know who I am.

I am loved beyond belief.

I am free to be alive.

I am a dreamer.

I am content.

I am confident.

I am selfless.

I am grateful.

I am forgiven.

I am worthy.

I am a child of the King.

I am a leader.

I am redeemed.

I am pure.

I am made new.

Though the list goes on and on, this is a brief glimpse of who I am able to be when Jesus speaks into my life. I always wonder what my life would look like without God in it, and I suppose it would just be the opposite of this list, but I also don't believe I'd be alive either. So I maybe should add that to the list. And I'm not saying I've achieved these qualities at any rate, but they are something I'm constantly pursuing and running toward because of who Jesus says I am. You'd be surprise how much your life can change when you start listening to what Jesus has to say about you and not what the world is yelling at you.

I hope my words challenged you and opened your eyes to a deeper way of living life, one that has meaning and purpose. God called us to something more than the American-dream mentality. You were made for so much more. In some way, shape, or form, I pray this book impacted you in a life-altering way. When we join God through his invitation to live a better story, we gain momentum along the way, leading us to a place we never imagined could be this life-sustaining.

Give life away. Be like Jesus.

FOLLOW DEREK

www.derekgarde.com
Instagram: dare__wreck
www.facebook.com/derekgarde